KITSAP REGIONAL LIBRARY
3 9068 00644 5045
D0852044
DATE DU

The World of the POLAR BEAR

Thor Larsen

The World of the POLAR BEAR

With a Foreword by
Sir Peter Scott CBE DSC
Honorary Chairman WWF International Council

CHARTWELL BOOKS, INC.

Foreword

It is a pleasant task to write a foreword for a book about the conservation of Polar Bears, because it is a success story that illustrates how people and governments can work together for a common cause.

The Polar Bear, awesome symbol of the Arctic, lived a relatively undisturbed life until a few decades ago. It was hunted by the Eskimos for its pelt, meat and other products, while whalers and sealers also killed some bears. But on the whole the Polar Bear had most of the Arctic to itself. The 1950s saw a big change, for technological developments during the Second World War made vehicles and other equipment available which enabled men to penetrate further into the Arctic. Trophy hunting developed on a large scale in Alaska and Svalbard, with boats and aircraft helping the hunter get his prey. The demand for Polar Bear skins began to grow so that traditional hunters found it profitable to hunt for the market instead of merely for subsistence. In Svalbard, coal-miners could make a useful spare-time profit by using the 'set-gun', a trap in which the Polar Bear triggers a rifle to shoot itself when taking the bait.

The Polar Bear was thus an obvious candidate when the IUCN (International Union for Conservation of Nature and Natural Resources) began to compile its *Red Data Book* of endangered species.

At that time we knew very little about the animal, its distribution in the Arctic, its numbers, and how it lived. Soviet experts thought there were about 5–8,000 bears, while the Americans suggested that there might be 20,000. It was thought that Polar Bears probably constituted a single population which migrated around the Arctic circle.

Arising from the growing concern about the Polar Bear's future, expressed by the Survival Service Commission of IUCN, the United States convened a meeting in Fairbanks, Alaska, in 1965, of specialists from the five circumpolar nations: the Soviet Union, Norway, Canada, Denmark and itself. This was followed in 1968 by a meeting at Morges, Switzerland, under the auspices of the SSC, which led to the establishment of a Polar Bear Specialist Group. The scientists involved, among whom Dr Thor Larsen was a prominent figure, co-ordinated their research work in order to build up a clear picture of Polar Bear dynamics as a basis for conservation measures.

The annual take of Polar Bears reached 1,300 in 1970, but fortunately the co-ordinated conservation effort began to take effect and hunting was brought under control everywhere within national sovereignties. However, there remained the international waters and the ice packs and, following a Soviet appeal for international control, IUCN prepared draft proposals and Norway convened a crucial meeting in Oslo in 1973, at which an agreement on the conservation of Polar Bears was completed. Thus, the Polar Bear has received overall protection from man the hunter – except for traditional harvesting by local peoples, which is still permitted.

I wish we could now sit back and say that we have thus saved the Polar Bear. Unhappily there remain some insidious and dangerous threats, most important of which is the increasing exploration of the High Arctic for oil and other minerals, which brings the disturbance of men and machines and the dangers of pollution to areas where Polar Bears live, including critical denning areas where the young are born. A start has been made in establishing national parks and other conservation areas, but more will be required to minimize this new human impact.

At the same time pesticides and other chemical pollutants used far away from the Arctic have found their way there and can be traced in Polar Bear tissues. Their potential for damage cannot yet be estimated.

The success of the effort to conserve the Polar Bear has been gratifying for all concerned. Similar international efforts have saved the Vicuña of the High Andes from imminent extinction, and given the Tiger a new lease of life in Asia. They all illustrate the way in which IUCN and WWF (World Wildlife Fund) are able to achieve conservation of our natural heritage by bringing together specialists, organizations and nations in the common cause, and to provide financial support when required.

But this financial support depends on donations from the public and it is pleasant to be able so say that buying this book will help, because Dr Larsen is generously making all his royalties available to WWF for further Polar Bear research.

Peter Scott.

Preface

This book is based not only upon my own observations and research, which I began in the mid-1960s. Far greater in importance is the data and information provided by others who have been occupied with Polar Bears and Arctic ecology either as professionals or because of a genuine interest in nature, biology and the polar regions. In particular I want to thank my Norwegian colleagues and friends Magnar Norderhaug and Nils Øritsland for their cooperation and advice over several years. Polar Bear trappers, hunters and weather-station crews have collected material and data and given me important information. The major reason for the success of the field expeditions is due to the work and effort of the crews of the ships and aircraft, as well as my assistants who never had to be asked twice for help. The Sysselmann (Governor) of Svalbard has always been most helpful. Tore Gjelsvik, the Director of The Norwegian Polar Institute has, more than anybody else, helped to launch Polar Bear research in Norway. Odd Lønø's great experience and knowledge has been a great help to me. I also want to thank my colleagues in other countries, Albert W. Erickson, Vagn Flyger, Marty Schein and Ivars Silis, whom I have had the pleasure to work with both in the field and in the laboratory. The inspiration and advice I have received from my colleagues and friends in the IUCN Polar Bear Specialist Group has been very important to me. The Group members are George Kolenosky (Canada), Jack W. Lentfer (USA), Ian Stirling (Canada), John Tener (Canada), Savva M. Uspensky (USSR), and Christian Vibe (Denmark). Former members are A. G. Bannikov (USSR), Jim Brooks (USA), Olav Hjeljord (Norway), Chuck Jonkel (Canada), Sasha Kistshchinski (USSR), A. H. Macpherson (Canada), and Eigil Reimers (Norway). Ian Stirling and Christian Vibe have reviewed the manuscript for this book, for which I am very grateful.

The support from the IUCN and the WWF has always been highly appreciated. Without the efforts and support from those two organizations, the progress in international Polar Bear research and conservation would not have been possible.

T. L.

Contents

First published in Great Britain in 1978 by
The Hamlyn Publishing Group Limited,
a Division of the Octopus Publishing Group,
Michelin House, 81 Fulham Road,
London SW3 6RB, England

This 1989 edition published by
Chartwell Books, Inc.
a division of Book Sales, Inc.,
110 Enterprise Avenue,
Secaucus, New Jersey 07094

ISBN 1-55521-416-9

Produced by Mandarin Offset
Printed and bound in Hong Kong

Introduction

Different landscapes and natural habitats throughout the world are almost always characterized by different animals and plants. The symbol of the African savannah is the Lion (*Panthera leo*), and that of the southeast Asian tropical rainforest is the Tiger (*Panthera tigris*). The Vicuña (*Vicugna vicugna*) symbolizes the South American Andes mountains, while the kangaroo (*Macropus* spp.) is typical of the Australian plains. Antarctica has its penguins (*Aptenodytes* spp.), but the symbol of the northern polar regions must surely be the Polar Bear (*Ursus maritimus*). This huge carnivore occurs on emblems of Arctic expeditions and enterprises of various sorts, on tourist brochures and on book dust-jackets.

An encounter with a Polar Bear in its natural habitat is a high priority for most people who visit the Arctic, whether they are tourists who occasionally visit the Far North, or scientists who regularly come in touch with the animal. Over the years that I have specialized in Arctic biology and with Polar Bears in particular, I have encountered many hundreds of bears and I have found every such meeting to be filled with both joy and awe. Every time, I am struck by the beauty and strength of this heavy and yet elegant animal. The more I learn about the biology and life history of the Polar Bear, the more interesting I find it.

Every encounter with the Polar Bear is different, but some I remember particularly well. Some years ago, I spent one year involved with Polar Bear research in the eastern Svalbard (Spitsbergen) area. I lived with three companions at a small station from which we often travelled to trappers' cabins and huts where we worked for long periods making observations and field studies. During January, I was staying alone in a trapper's cabin on Halvmåneøya (Halfmoon Island) which is famous among Norwegian Polar Bear hunters for its abundance of bears at certain times of the year. I was there for two weeks to study bear migration and behaviour. I did not even have the dogs with me as I feared that they might disturb the bears and hamper my observations.

One biting cold morning, I found the tracks of a huge bear in the newly fallen snow just outside the door. An old male had passed the cabin sometime during the night. He had evidently paid little attention to the hut and to my equipment outside it. The tracks which came straight in from the frozen sea-ice, went past the hut and straight over to the other side of the island, where there were some leads (open channels through an ice-field) and other opportunities for the bear to catch seals.

Soon afterwards I was dressed and had my skis on, and was on his tracks. A white camouflage suit gave me good cover among the ice hummocks, and I hoped to be able to get close to him and to make some observations of his seal-catching methods. To begin with, the tracks were easy to follow. Big as the bottoms of buckets, they made a wide trail across the shore-ice towards the pressure ridges and hummocks further south. The long fur on the bear's chest and heels had swept the newly fallen snow. But out in the broken ice the tracks became more difficult to follow. They went back and forth, following a pressure ridge, then crossing a field with newly frozen ice, where only the clawmarks were visible, and where I had sometimes to search carefully to find his path. In places, the bear had worked his way through deep snowdrifts, leaving a trail like that of a small vehicle. Sometimes the tracks went to the top of a high iceberg, where the bear would have looked around for open leads and seals.

I had to be careful in this chaos of pressure ridges, icebergs, hummocks and frozen floes. In such a broken terrain I might suddenly find myself face to face with the bear. If thus surprised, the animal might find itself cornered and if the

These tracks show a successful 'seal kill' by a Polar Bear. The seal had been resting by a blowhole when the bear stalked up to it and then with a very swift charge, jumped upon it.

distance was short, he might attack; I knew that such an attack would be sudden and very swift.

I had been on the bear's trail for more than two hours when I discovered him. I was on the top of a pressure ridge when I suddenly spotted his pale yellow fur, which easily distinguished him from the very white surroundings. The bear had walked in a wide circle and picked up my ski trail, which he was now following. He was also being very careful, moving only a few steps at a time, mostly with his nose down low on my trail. But occasionally he raised his head and sniffed the air. Fortunately I was hidden behind a large mound of ice, and down-wind of the bear. Thus I could follow his movements without arousing his suspicion.

Polar Bears always impress me when I meet them in their natural element, their bodies often seem heavy and even somewhat clumsy but they walk with an almost cat-like elegance, the head and the long neck slowly moving from side to side or up and down, as they try to catch the scent of any foreign object. Polar Bears have relatively poor eyesight, but a very good

Above
The pack-ice is the true domain of the Polar Bear.

sense of smell. Most of the year the pelt is creamy white, with long hairs that are bright and shiny. Even if the Polar Bear usually seems slow or even docile, it can move with surprising speed. Then the body seems loaded with energy and strength, and in a few explosive cat-like jumps the huge carnivore is upon its prey. It is rather helpless in the water though it is a strong but slow swimmer, which can keep going for hours. However, it can be easily overtaken by a rowboat, or even a good human swimmer. The bear cannot take seals in the water, as they are too swift for it and, unlike the seals, the bear cannot dive very deep or for long.

The bear came steadily closer. He was a magnificent specimen, close to half a ton, and with a beautiful shining coat. His breath formed small clouds in the cold air. I could hear his sniffing, and the crunching of the snow as he worked his way through a snowdrift.

When he was less than twenty metres (sixty-six feet) away, I whistled softly. The big animal stopped immediately and raised his head. He sniffed the air, and moved his head back and forth to get my scent. Then he saw me. He stood still for a moment, then lowered his head and blew the air out through his nose with great force, thus signalling a warning. He walked slowly backwards a few paces, smacking his teeth – another typical warning, which signals that one should not try to get closer. Then suddenly he threw himself around and jumped away, throwing snow to both sides as he made his way through the deep snow. Soon afterwards he had disappeared among the pressure ridges.

Above
Polar Bears are not fast runners. They become exhausted if pursued for some time. Travellers on snowmachines or in boats should remember this, as the bears can be harmed if pursued intensively.

Left
Polar Bears are slow swimmers, but can often keep swimming for days. Observations have been made of Polar Bears as far away from their natural habitat as the Norwegian coast, Iceland and even Japan.

Early encounters with man

As long as Man has lived and travelled in the Arctic Polar Bears have been hunted, mainly for their beautiful, creamy shining pelt. The Vikings regarded Polar Bear pelts as precious items; they were considered extraordinary also in Medieval Europe. Together with Walrus (*Odobenus rosmarus*) tusks, Greenland Falcons (*Falco rusticolus*) and various furs, Polar Bear pelts were the most important export items for the descendants of Eirik the Red in Greenland. In 1274 the Arabian author Ibn Said wrote about Denmark and Greenland:

'Westwards [of Denmark] is the island of the white falcons . . . . . and from there white falcons are taken to the sultan of Egypt, who pays 1000 dinars for them out of his treasuries . . . . and here are the white bears. Those bear hides are soft, and they are taken to Egypt as gifts . . . .'

Even in Norway, Polar Bear hides were considered very rare. Troels-Lund wrote that

'. . . there was a custom to send the pelts from Polar Bears to the archbishop in Trondheim as a gift of gratitude. Thus, there were Polar Bear rugs in front of all altars in the cathedral, so that the clerics should not have cold feet when they were reading the early mass.'

Live Polar Bears were regarded as extraordinary treasures, which were reserved for kings and emperors. Several Norwegian fairy tales report about white bears which were taken to the King to be sold, or to be given away.

Killing a bear has in ancient, as well as in modern times, been considered one of the most distinguished feats of sportmanship in Greenland. Eirik the Red is said to have quarreled with one of his best friends from envy on account of the latter having had the luck to capture a bear. About the year 1060 an Icelander named Audun came to Greenland and gave all his property in exchange for a living bear, which he brought as a present to King Svend in Denmark, who gave Audun in reward an honourable maintenance for life. The king, also, discharged his chamberlain because he tried to extort money from Audun for being admitted to the king.

With the primitive weapons of our ancestors and the Eskimos, it is understandable why Polar Bears were treasured. In Medieval times Polar Bears had to be hunted with spears, in very much the same way as Brown Bears (*Ursus arctos*) were hunted in Europe at that time, or the big cats were hunted in other parts of the world. The Eskimos used to hunt bears with assistance from their dogs. When a bear was seen, or a fresh track was found, the dogs were turned loose, and if they were properly trained, they soon surrounded the big carnivore. In such situations, the bear would be forced to fight the dogs, using his mighty paws to try and slap or grab his enemies. While the bear was occupied with the dogs, the hunter could approach with his spear or lance at the ready, and stab the beast to death. However, bears are incredibly swift and strong animals, and such hunts could be very risky, because the hunter could do little, should the bear suddenly leap upon him. The Thule Eskimos from Greenland claimed that Polar Bears were only able to strike with their left paw. Therefore, it was less dangerous for the hunter to approach the animal from the left. The Eskimos point out that the Polar Bear shown on the seal of the Royal Greenland Trade Company is not correct: it has raised the right forepaw, as if ready to strike.

The Eskimos still use dogs in their Polar Bear hunts, but the spear and the lance have been replaced by the gun. But even if the hunting has changed, and Eskimo tribes have undergone great social and cultural changes during the last few decades, Eskimo hunters still consider Polar Bear hunting a test of manhood. Until recently, a young man of the Thule Eskimos of northwest Greenland was not worthy of the daughter of a great hunter

Above
Summer hunting by means of kayak. An experienced hunter can use a gun as well as a harpoon from the kayak, and take seals, Walruses and Narwhals.

Left
Polar Bears are often curious, and they will often rise on their hind legs in order to get a better look. In this case, it is a vessel which has stirred the bear's curiosity.

Eskimos travel by dog sledge and, more recently, by snow-machines in winter, but prefer the light and easily manoeuvrable kayak in summer. In many areas, Eskimo hunters are almost totally dependent upon their kayaks.

until he had killed his first bear. Polar Bear hides are still used for trousers and other everyday items by many Eskimos, although many are also tanned and sold to fur-trade companies and tourists. But many Eskimos claim that there is no synthetic material which can match the Polar Bear's fur when it comes to making strong, warm and durable trousers for the Arctic traveller and hunter.

Polar Bears and mythology

The Polar Bear has a very special place in Eskimo mythology and culture. There were many taboos connected to the Polar Bear, as the following examples show.

An Eskimo tells:

'The Polar Bear is a dangerous animal, but we need it. We must hunt it and kill it, but we also have to take some precautions so that the bear's soul will not return and harm us.

The bears hear everything and know everything Man talks about.

When the bear hunter returns with his prey, the bear hide must be taken into the house and put in a "krimerfix", which is a case where the dog-food is stored.

If it is a male bear, one must hang a rope over the bear's nose, and in the rope there must be a harpoon, some blubber and meat and some pieces of leather. Everything is for the bear's soul. The leather is for the repair of the bear's boots, because a bear walks a lot.

If it is a female bear, only a piece of tanned seal hide, some meat and some pieces of leather are hung over its hide.

Everything must remain like this for at least five days. Furthermore, all bones from the bear must be collected as its meat is eaten, and the bones must be piled up by the skull, in the window-frame. The skull must face inwards.

All this is done in order to help the bear find its home. The bear gets human tools and equipment, because bears can often change themselves into humans.'

It was sometimes claimed that the bears came to the humans voluntarily because they wanted gifts from the hunters. After treated as mentioned above, and offered gifts, the bear would bring the gifts with him when born anew in another skin and another flesh. Some said that after the bear's skull, hide and bones have been in the house for five days – these were the bear's visiting days – and received gifts, the skull should be boiled and thrown into the sea. Only thus treated, could the bear return home.

When rare animals such as Narwhals (*Monodon monoceros*), Walruses and Polar Bears were caught at an Eskimo village, a father would rub his son with an amulet made with the skin of a seal's head, filled with seaweed. Thus, his son would be able to catch similar game animals.

It was commonly believed that when somebody ate Polar Bear meat and lost the piece of meat on the floor, he could not pick it up right away. He had to pick it up

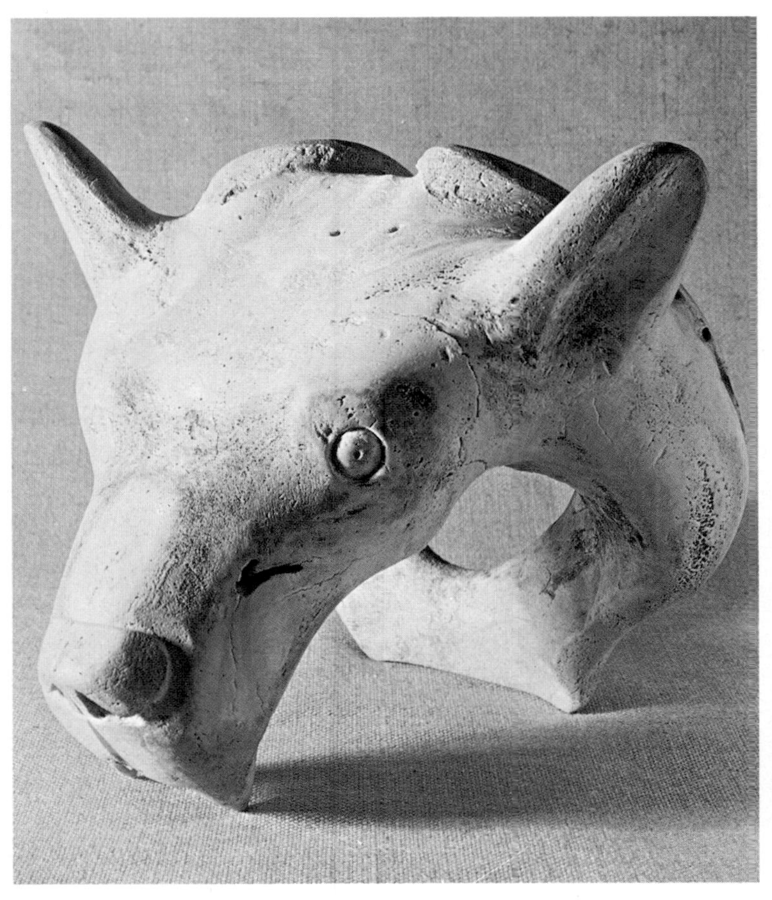

Above
This is a 'bear spirit' from the Canadian Arctic, carved from a whale vertebrae; the human face on the back is the feminine one of a pair.

Left
This is a beautiful bear family made from Greenstone. By Pauta, Cape Dorset, Northwest Territories.

from behind the legs, beneath his crooked knee, if not, he would himself be eaten by a bear.

Several Eskimo legends and myths tell about Polar Bears which were able to change themselves into human beings. Often such bears lived by themselves in a house, inside which they became human but outside remain as bears. Sometimes humans came to these houses, and were often well treated as long as they were inside. But they had to take care outside, and were forced to flee for their lives in order not to be killed by the bears. As an example, there is the story of the origin of the constellation Canis Major – the Great Dog:

'A woman once ran away from her family and after a while she came upon a house. By the entrance there were several Polar Bear hides, despite this she went inside. The house belonged to some bears which were able to change into humans. The woman decided to stay with them. A big bear caught food for the household; when he went hunting he would put on his bear skin. One day the woman wished to return home to see her family. The big bear agreed but told her not to talk of her experiences as he was frightened that his two cubs would be killed. The woman went home, but could not remain silent about the bears. One evening while she was sitting with her husband she whispered, "I have seen bears". The men of the village immediately drove out and when the bear saw them coming he feared what might happen to his cubs and killed them both as he did not want the humans to have them.

Then the bear took off in search of the woman who had betrayed them. He

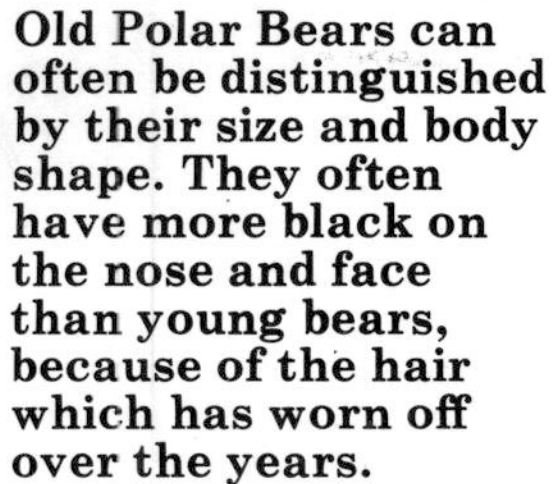

Old Polar Bears can often be distinguished by their size and body shape. They often have more black on the nose and face than young bears, because of the hair which has worn off over the years.

found her house, broke in and killed her. As he came out the dogs closed in on him and started to attack. Suddenly, as the bear was defending himself, they all became lights and rose into the sky where they became stars. Today we call them *Krilugtussat:* they who resemble a pack of dogs barking after a bear.

After that, the humans were careful with the bears, because they hear what the humans say.'

Parallel stories about bears which can change into humans can be found in Nordic mythology and fairy tales. An example is the story of *The White bear, King Valemon:*

'Once upon a time there was a King, who had three daughters. Two were ugly and evil, but the third was pure and good, and the King and everybody else loved her. She once dreamed about a wreath of gold, and once as she walked in the forest she met a white bear which had the wreath she had dreamt about. She offered to buy it, but the bear would not part with it, unless she would stay with him. She could not live without the wreath and so she agreed that the bear should come for her in three days, which happened to be Thursday. The bear came, and the army was sent out to stop him, but in vain, and finally the King sent out his oldest daughter to the bear. He took her on his back and ran off. After a long ride he asked her: "Did you ever sit more softly, did you ever see further?" "Yes, in my mother's lap did I sit more softly, and from my father's castle did I see further," was the answer. "Then you are not the right one," frowned the bear and chased her back home.

The next Thursday he was back, and although the army fought braver than last time, they could not stop him, and the King sent out his second daughter. The same thing happened. After a long ride, the bear asked the princess: "Did you ever sit more softly, and did you ever see further?" "Yes, in my mother's lap did I sit more softly, and from my father's castle did I see further," was the answer. "Then you are not the right one," growled the bear and chased her away.

The third time the bear came, the army fought braver than ever, but had to give in at last, and the King had to send out his youngest daughter. After a long ride through the forest, the bear asked her the same questions he had asked the two others. "No never!" she said. "Then you are the right one," said the bear. He took her away to his castle, where she was to stay with him. The bear was away during daytime, but at nights he was with her, and then he was human.'

There are similarities with the Eskimo tale mentioned above. The princess asks to go home to visit her parents and sisters, and reluctantly, the bear agrees, provided she will not listen to the advice from her mother. But the mother convinces the princess to take a candle with her, which she can light so that she can see her partner while he is asleep at night. Thus the princess discovers that the bear is a beautiful prince. But as she leans forward to kiss him, wax drips from the candle on to him and wakes him. The prince tells her that a witch has changed him into a Polar Bear. The princess might have saved him from the spell, but because of her disobedience, he has to leave her to marry the witch. But the princess cannot give him up. Through many sacrifices and difficulties she is able to find him again. By doing this she is able to help him get rid of the witch and they are able to marry each other. Thus, the tale has a happy ending, as most fairy tales do.

Polar Bears and early explorers

Old expedition diaries and journals often picture Polar Bears as dangerous and ferocious beasts, capable of damaging equipment and killing people. With the primitive weapons and equipment the first explorers had to rely upon, Polar Bears undoubtedly represented a real danger in certain situations. When Willem Barents tried to sail the northeast seaway in 1596, and thereby discovered Spitsbergen, he and his crew fought a Polar Bear off the island which today is known as Björnöya (Bear Island) – named after that incident. Old etchings show Barents' men in two small boats, fighting a bear which is swimming in the water. Gerrit de Veer wrote:

'The twelfth of June in the morning: we saw a white bear, which we rowed after with our boat, thinking to cast a rope about her neck; but when we were near her, she was so great that we durst not do it, but rowed back again to our ship to fetch more men and our arms; and so made to her again with muskets, hargubushes, halbertes, and hatchets; John Cornellyson's men coming also with their boat to help us. And so being well furnished of men and weapons, we rowed with both our boats unto the bear, and fought with her while four glasses were run out, for our weapons could do her little hurt; and amongst the rest of the blows that we gave her, one of our men stroke her into the back with an axe, which stuck fast in her back, and yet she swam away with it; but we rowed after her, and at last we cut her head in sunder with an axe, wherewith she died; and then we brought her into John Cornellyson's ship, where we fleaed her, and found her skin to be twelve foot long: which done, we ate some of her flesh; but we brookt it not well. This island we called the Bear Island.'

The year before, two of Barents' men had been killed by a bear. The accident happened as follows, according to de Veer:

'The sixth of September: some of our men went on shore upon the firm land so to seek for stones, which are a kind of diamond, whereof there are many also in the States Island, and while they were seeking the stones, two of our men lying together in one place, a great lean white bear came suddenly stealing out, and caught one of them fast by the neck, who not knowing what it was that took him by the neck, cried out and said, "Who is that who pulls me so by the neck?' Wherewith the other, that lay not far from him, lifted up his head to see who it was, and perceiving it to be a monsterous bear, cried and said, "Oh mate, it is a bear!" and therewith presently rose up and ran away.

The bear at the first falling upon the man, bit his head in sunder, and sucked out his blood, wherewith the rest of the men that were on land, being about twenty in number, ran presently thither, either to save the man, or else to drive the bear from the dead body; and having charged their pieces and bent their pikes, set upon her, that still was devouring the man, but she perceiving them to come towards her, fiercely and cruelly ran at them, and gat another of them out from the company, which she tore in pieces, wherewith all the rest ran away.

We perceiving out of our ship and pinace that our men ran to the sea-side to save themselves, with all speed entered into our boats, and rowed as fast as we could to the shore to relieve our men. Where being on land, we beheld the cruel spectacle of our two dead men, that had been so cruelly killed and torn in pieces by the bear. We seeing that, incouraged our men to go back again with us, and with pieces, courtlaxes, and half-pikes, to set upon the bear; but they would not all agree thereunto, some of them saying, "Our men are already dead, and we shall get the bear well enough, though we oppose not ourselves into so open danger; if we might save our fellows' lives, then we would make haste; but now we need not make such speed, but take her at an advantage, with most security for ourselves, for we have to do with a cruel, fierce and ravenous beast. Whereupon three of our men went forward, the bear still devouring her prey, not once fearing the number of our men, and yet they were thirty at the least: the three that went forward in that sortie, were Cornelius Jacobson, master of Willem Barents' ship, Willem Geysen, pilot of the pinace, and Hans van Nufflen, Willem Barents' purser: and after that the said master and pilot shot three times and missed, the purser stepping somewhat further forward, and seeing the bear to be within the length of a shot, presently levelled his piece, and discharging it at the bear, shot her into the head between both the eyes, and yet she held the man still fast by the neck, and lifted up her head, with the man in her mouth, but she began somewhat to stagger; wherewith the purser and a Scotishman drew out their courtlaxes, and stroke at her so hard that their courtlaxes burst, and yet she would not leave the man. At last Willem Geysen went to them, and with all his might stroke the bear upon the snout with his piece, at which time the bear fell to the ground, making a great noise, and Willem Geysen leaping upon her cut her throat. The seventh of September we buried the dead bodies of our men in the States Island, and having fleaed the bear, carried her skin to Amsterdam.'

The Norwegian explorer and scientist Fridtjof Nansen has described another dangerous incident with a Polar Bear:

'During the German expedition to the east coast of Greenland in 1869–1870 it twice happened that men were attacked by bears. On one occasion one of the scientists, Börgen, was even dragged away for a considerable distance. It was on a winter's night, and he had been out to read the thermometers, which were set up on shore at a little distance from the ship. He was coming back when he heard something padding along behind him. He turned round and found himself face to face with a bear. He had no time to cock the gun which he had with him, so he tried to frighten the bear by thrusting his bull's-eye lantern into its face, but the animal without taking any notice of this knocked Börgen over, bit him twice in the head, and dragged him off. His cries for help were heard on the ship, and his comrades rushed to his aid. Shots were fired to frighten the beast, which dropped Börgen and moved off a couple of paces, but came back again and towed him on over the uneven ice at a gallop. At last it let him go and took to flight.

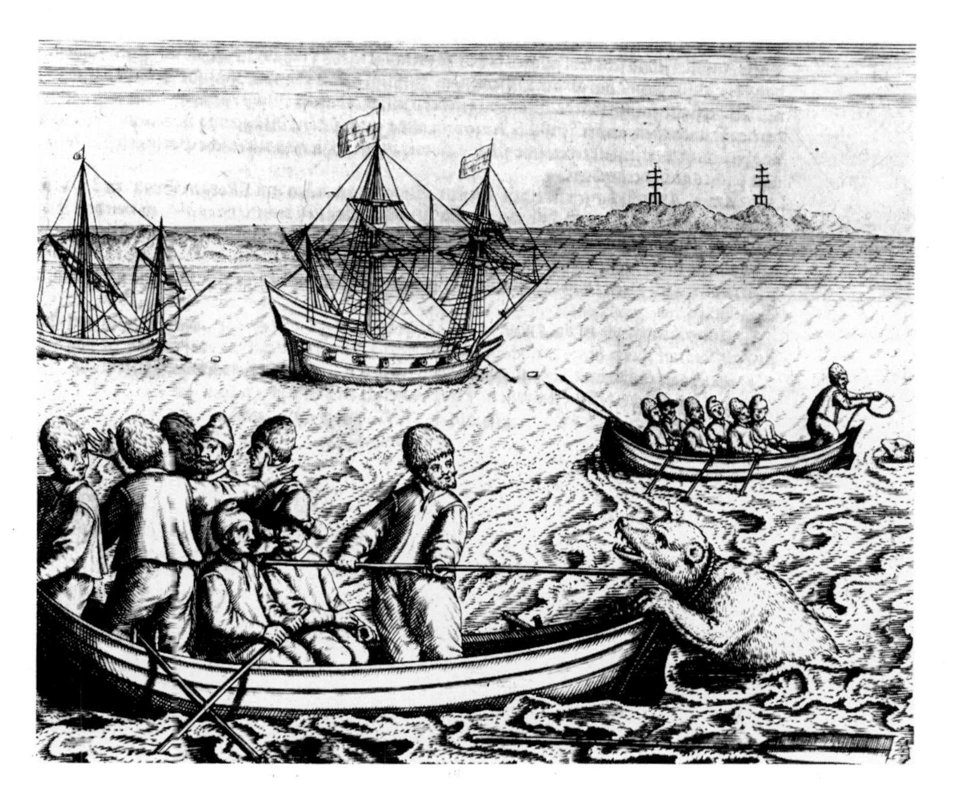

Top
One of Barents' men has managed to slip a noose around a Polar Bear's neck. The other sailors are either trying to balance the boat or are more probably keeping their distance. From an engraving by Theodore de Bry.

Middle
Barents and his men on Novaya Zemlya in May 1597. Notice the cabin is surrounded by animal traps which are very similar to those still used today (see p.59).

Left
An eighteenth-century engraving of an encounter with a Polar Bear.

Early explorers and Arctic travellers depicted Polar Bears as vicious and very dangerous animals. Today we know that this huge carnivore is often the most gentle of the bear species.

Above
'The animal knocked Börgen over, bit him twice in the head, and dragged him off. His cries for help were heard on the ship, and his comrades rushed to his aid.'

Below
Horatio Nelson, participating in Phipps expedition to the North in 1773 at the age of fifteen, experienced a dramatic encounter with a Polar Bear.

Börgen was seriously injured, but recovered. His thick fur cap had saved his head from too severe damage from the bites.'

In his book *Hunting and adventure in the Arctic*, Fridtjof Nansen wrote extensively about the Polar Bear. He made many observations and statements about Polar Bear biology, which have been verified by modern research a hundred years later. About its ferocity, Nansen wrote:

'As regards the courage of the bear and the extent to which it is to be feared, opinions vary greatly. Some authorities have made it out to be quite harmless, while others have drawn exaggerated pictures of its ferocity. In old accounts of travels in the Arctic seas, it is often depicted as a terrible monster, which attacks and kills man after man, and for fighting which, large parties of men have to be called out.'

Nansen correctly pointed out that the bear's behaviour towards man to a large degree depends upon the circumstances where the bear is met and pointed out that bears often approach man, not necessarily with the intention of attacking. Nansen wrote:

'. . . . it is probably more a case of curiosity, it wants to find out what this creature may be, so it comes slowly, shambling along and stares and sniffs, after a while it may wander off again, if it is not shot. . . . .

If the bear has enough food, and is not disturbed, I do not believe that it will attack human beings. On the Saddlebacks' (*Pagophilus groenlandicus*) breeding-grounds it can be quite friendly. It has often come and sniffed at the piles of skins, and gone off again without showing any hostile design. The men stood by and watched; they had not as a rule any rifles with them, but only seal-clubs, which are not much of a weapon to tackle a bear with.

On one occasion my helmsman, Kristian "Balloon", during the slaughter of the young seals had just collected together as many skins as he could tow, had got the drag-rope made fast, and was just about to harness himself to the load for the journey home, when a bear came and sniffed at his skins. He took no notice of the bear, but proceeded homewards with his freight. The bear followed close at his heels, and thus they came marching forwards towards the ship, the "Balloon" in front with the skins, and the bear jogging good-temperedly after, until at the approach of men running from the ship with rifles, it took its departure.'

But Nansen was to experience that Polar Bears could be dangerous. During his transpolar expedition with the ship '*Fram*', one of his men was attacked by a Polar Bear. Peder Henriksen had been down on the ice to check some instruments, and on his way back to the ship, he suddenly discovered a shadow in the darkness, close by. Thinking it was one of the dogs, he did not take any notice of the animal, before it suddenly bit him in the hip. Henriksen slammed the headlamp in the bear's head, and got away. But Nansen himself was part of a much more dangerous incident when he and Johansen tried to reach the North Pole by skis and sledge in the spring. Nansen writes:

'. . . . I heard a scuffle behind me, and Johansen, who had just turned round to

pull his sledge flush with mine, cried, "Take the gun!" I turned round and saw an enormous bear throwing itself on him, and Johansen on his back. I tried to seize my gun, which was in the case on the foredeck, but at the same moment the kayak slipped into the water. My first thought was to throw myself into the water over the kayak and fire from there, but I recognized how risky it would be. I began to pull the kayak with its heavy cargo on to the high edge of the ice again as quickly as I could, and was on my knees pulling and tugging to get at my gun. I had no time to look round and see what was going on behind me, when I heard Johansen quietly say: "You must look sharp if you want to be in time". Look sharp? I should think so! At last I got hold of the butt end, dragged the gun out, turned round in the sitting posture, and cocked the shot-barrel. The bear was standing not one metre [two yards] off, ready to make an end of my dog "Kaifas". There was no time to lose in cocking the other barrel, so I gave it a charge of shot behind the ear, and it fell down dead between us.'

Other incidents have a more happy ending. A Norwegian sealing skipper, Kulstad, reports a curious story, from about a hundred years ago, about the way his brother got away from an attacking bear in a somewhat peculiar way, namely by singing the national anthem for the bear. The man had been separated from his companions, and was returning to them across the sea-ice when he found himself pursued by a bear. He tried to get away, but as the bear was much faster than him, he soon found the situation so critical that he turned around and prepared to defend himself with his knife – the only weapon he had. The bear stopped – the man ran away, and the bear followed him again and got unpleasantly close. 'Soon the bear had taken up the pursuit, and was on his heels', reads Kulstad's diary. 'He then began to sing the national anthem, which made the bear sit down and listen, and it remained sitting in that position until he had got so far away that he believed he could not be overtaken by the bear. However, the bear followed him all the way to the shore, now and then stopping in order to listen to the song, and thus he was saved.'

It is well known that Polar Bears which pursue humans may be distracted by sounds or various items which are thrown down on the ground. The Canadian Federal Provincial Bear Committee has issued a poster which advises people how to act when encountering a Polar Bear. Among other things it reads: 'If chased, throw your toque, parca, pack etc. to divert the bear's attention. Then *run!*' This is undoubtedly good advice. Bears are easily

Few animal pelts can match the Polar Bear in beauty and strength. Polar Bear rugs have been considered as gifts for kings and emperors. Eskimo hunters claim that the best trousers are made from Polar Bear hides.

Polar Bears examine almost everything unusual, and may cause considerable harm to unguarded depots, camps and vehicles.

distracted unless they have started a true attack. But many who have travelled in the Arctic have experienced that if one immediately turns the back to a bear and runs away when approached, the animal will most likely follow out of plain curiosity, or because the fleeing human may trigger an instinct to chase the object.

One very peculiar story, about an encounter with a Polar Bear, is given by the famous Danish explorer and scientist Knud Rasmussen, who was once hunting with an Eskimo friend on the winter ice in Melville Bay in northwest Greenland. They came upon the fresh tracks of a Polar Bear, and started to hunt the animal. After a swift chase with the dog team, Rasmussen saw the bear and let the dogs loose. Meanwhile, his Eskimo friend had got into some trouble with his dogs, and was left behind. The situation was perfect for Rasmussen as he was alone on the hunt, and he enjoyed it, because among the Greenland Eskimos the Polar Bear is a true challenge for dog-drivers and hunters.

Rasmussen had to get close in order to avoid shooting the dogs. He was only six metres (twenty feet) from the snarling bear and the fighting dogs, when the beast discovered him. Sometimes, when Polar Bears are met with on thin ice, they may try to break the ice and get into the sea. With forceful jumps and the full downwards thrust of its heavy body, the animal often succeeded in this manoeuvre. And this was exactly what happened this time. Rasmussen's bear succeeded in its effort to break the ice which was thinner than Rasmussen had expected and not only did the bear fall in the open water, but so did the man. Rasmussen made several efforts to crawl on to the ice again, but it only broke under him. He tried to throw his rifle on to the ice, but lost it, and the gun slipped into the water.

Rasmussen gradually became colder, and he soon ceased to spend his energy in vain in trying to get out on to the ice. He was in an extremely dangerous situation. Not only was he about to freeze to death in the icy water, but he also had to watch the bear which was only a short distance away as it swam slowly about, snarling towards him and the dogs, which were standing on the ice, waiting for the bear to come out of the water. Eventually the bear discovered that the dogs never attacked Rasmussen. And after some time, it slowly swam closer to him as if to seek protection there from the dogs. As Rasmussen understood the problems which would arise if the dogs came closer to them both, he shouted to the dogs to keep away. So a unique situation had been established. Now Rasmussen and the bear – the hunter and the hunted – were sticking close together in their common desperate situation. Rasmussen was getting more and more numb, and he knew that the rescue had to come soon, should he have any chance. And he promised to himself, that if he ever survived this, the bear should not be shot. Finally, Rasmussen's Eskimo friend Qolutanguaq came to his rescue. As Rasmussen was hauled on to the ice, he managed to whisper to his friend, 'Do not shoot the bear!' before he fainted.

He woke up warm and comfortable in his sleeping bag, and when his friend had a cup of hot tea ready for him, Rasmussen's first thought was for the bear: 'Where was the bear?' he asked. Qolutanguaq smiled at his friend. 'Do not bother about the bear', he said, 'it is already skinned.'

Are Polar Bears dangerous?

Apart from the stories in the preceeding chapter, it must be emphasized that Polar Bears do occasionally kill people. This will normally only happen, however, when bears are provoked or when they are extremely hungry. There are few documented reports about bears which have attacked people. More recently, there have been some accidents with the Polar Bears in Canada. In 1966 a twelve-years-old boy was attacked by a Polar Bear at Fort Churchill. In 1967, another bear attacked two Indians in the same general area, and in 1968, an Eskimo youngster was killed by a third bear. All three bears were killed by police officers. After the accidents an autopsy of the bear which had attacked the boy in 1966 showed that it had been wounded by firearms earlier, on the same day as it attacked. The bullets, which had hit it in the face, the abdomen and the leg may have been triggering factors for the attack. Two accidents with Polar Bears also occurred in the Canadian Arctic in 1975.

In 1971 a crew member of the Bjørnøya weather station in Svalbard was killed by a young bear. The man, who had been unarmed, was on a field trip with a dog, when he was attacked by the bear. The reason for the attack is not known, but it is reasonable to assume that the presence of the dog associated with great hunger may have been triggering factors. The bear was killed later, and autopsy revealed that it was extremely lean.

In the Soviet Arctic, at least four people were killed and five were injured between 1930 and 1967.

Over the years, I have discovered that people's attitudes towards Polar Bears often change the more often they see them and get used to them. The first encounter is often characterized by fear. People keep at a good distance, and take cover as soon as the bear moves towards them. This is an understandable – and safe – reaction. But soon people judge the bears to be heavy, clumsy and relatively slow, and they discover that they do not attack. As a result the observer gets bolder; he stands only a short distance away and takes pictures; he feeds bears by hand from a ship or a cabin door; he walks around in Polar Bear areas without arms. This is a dangerous and very short-sighted attitude. But after some more time and experience, the observer knows what he can do and what he should avoid doing. A certain distance is required in order not to provoke the big carnivore. The animal's behaviour can be interpreted and understood, and precautions can be taken as the animal approaches; there should always be various avenues of retreat. The Canadian Wildlife Service has launched a slogan which plainly states that, 'A safe Polar Bear is a distant Polar Bear'. This is a simple rule, which should be remembered by anybody who encounters Polar Bears in the field.

Polar Bears are often curious. Something unusual like a trail left by a snowmachine may make them stop and follow the track for miles.

When immobilized with the drug 'Sernylan' the hind quarter is first affected. The bear can now be approached with some care.

Before Polar Bears attack, they will normally signal their intentions. A curious Polar Bear is often somewhat uncertain in its movements. It walks relatively slowly, often back and forth, and stops frequently. Its head moves up and down, and from side to side. A provoked bear behaves differently. It will seem much more determined, and will often signal warnings by blowing air through its nose, or by smacking its teeth together. The attack comes surprisingly fast. The animal seems very determined. The head is kept low, and the bear moves towards the intruder at a surprising speed. Sometimes it attacks in long, cat-like jumps, without uttering a sound, or perhaps groaning. The bear becomes a tremendous concentration of strength and power, and there is very little time left for escape. It may be necessary to kill the bear, but it is often difficult to shoot because of the speed of the attacking animal and because of the general confusion which often occurs.

I have experienced half a dozen attacks from Polar Bears myself, and I must admit that they have all been provoked. Most attacks have been triggered off by situations caused by myself or my colleagues. One such incident happened in Svalbard one winter. Nils, a fellow researcher, had a female bear and her two cubs in a cage outside our station. He had finished his measurements and studies, samples had been taken, and the bears had been marked, and could now be released. Nils was going to open the cage for them. He would stand on top of the cage, and pull out a steel pipe which would enable the bears to get out. About twenty metres (sixty-six feet) away, in front of the door of the station, I stood with a rifle, ready in case any problems arose. My assistant, Reidar, held the door open for us. As Nils pulled out the pipe, he jumped down on to the snow and walked

towards the station. Suddenly the mother bear was out of the cage. She turned towards us – and attacked instantly! I shouted, 'She is coming!' to Nils who started to run. I realized that I had no choice but to shoot. I aimed straight at her, squeezed the trigger, and '*click*' – the rifle did not fire! I do not remember clearly what happened next, but I believe I threw down the rifle and made a vigorous jump backwards. Somehow I got through the door, but the bear was just behind me. Luckily, Reidar understood the difficult situation. He had held the door open until Nils and I had stumbled inside, and then slammed it shut. The door hit the bear on her nose, so that she was flung aside. But we were safe. We heard her groan and sniff outside the door for a short while. Then her cubs started to moan. The mother bear got them out of the cage, and all three headed for the ice.

At first glance, Polar Bears may seem heavy and clumsy. But in their natural habitat they move with a surprising elegance and beauty.

Characteristics and distribution

Polar Bears are considered to be the largest carnivores in the world, matched perhaps only by the Kodiak Brown Bear (*Ursus arctos*). However, Polar Bears differ in size throughout their range. A fully grown Polar Bear male in Svalbard may weigh as much as 500 or 600 kilograms (1100 or 1320 pounds), and measure more than three metres (ten feet) from nose to tail. The female is somewhat smaller, and rarely weighs more than 350 kilograms (770 pounds), and is about 2·5 metres (8·2 feet) long. In Alaska, a male Polar Bear may weigh 700 kilograms (1540 pounds) or more. Here, also, females are smaller than the males.

Most bear species are adapted to a life in forests and mountains. Polar Bears belong to the pack-ice, and they have developed different characteristics from the other species through the evolution from common ancestors. The most striking difference is the pelt colour, which is creamy or almost pure white in the Polar Bear and dark brown or black in other species. Brown Bear (*Ursus arctos*) and Black Bear (*Ursus americanus*) fur is rather soft, while Polar Bear guard-hairs are shiny and almost glossy, with a dense layer of under-fur. There is, also, a thick subcutaneous layer of fat which provides extra insulation against cold. Polar Bear ears are smaller than on other bear species, and the shape of the face is also different. It has a more 'roman nose' and not the flat face with more pronounced front and cheeks, which is seen in Brown and Black Bears. The skull and the neck are also longer on Polar Bears.

A closer look at a Polar Bear confirms that it is a more carnivorous animal than the Brown or Black Bear. Polar Bear claws are relatively short and sharp, while the two other species have long claws that are more suitable for digging. Polar Bears use their claws to grab and hold their prey. The cheek teeth are sharper and more edged than on other bear species, and the canine teeth are more prominent – an indication of a more carnivorous diet. While the Polar Bear is a true carnivore, other bears have a more omnivorous diet and eat mainly roots, berries and other plant items.

But even if Polar Bears are different from other bear species in many respects, investigations have shown that they are genetically very closely related. Comparison between blood protein components in Polar Bears, Black Bears and Brown Bears show very little differences. In zoological gardens there are examples of cross-breeding between Polar Bears and Brown Bears. Their offspring have even been fertile – another proof that the two species are very closely related. Bears are also closely related to dogs, and they have common prehistoric ancestors.

Distribution

It is the High Arctic coastal areas and the drift ice areas which are the true Polar Bear habitat. Here the bears find the seals they depend upon, as well as adequate conditions for their dens. Suitable habitat is relatively common along the northeast Greenland coast and along west Greenland between Melville Bay and the Kane Basin. In Arctic Canada, Polar Bears are common on most of the islands and sounds in the Far North and along the coastal mainland areas between 65° and 80° North latitude. It is also found as far south as the lower Hudson and James Bays. In those last two areas, Polar Bears roam as far as 150 kilometres (90 miles) inland into the coniferous forests, where they live very differently from Polar Bears which belong to the

Above
A walking Polar Bear will often turn its paws inward, as demonstrated in this picture. This young animal is also somewhat curious, and lowers its head as it approaches the photographer.

Left
The Black Bear (*Ursus americanus*) belongs to the North American continent, and is found north to Alaska. It is mainly a forest-dwelling animal, and is smaller than Brown and Polar Bears.

A map of the Arctic showing the distribution of the Polar Bear.

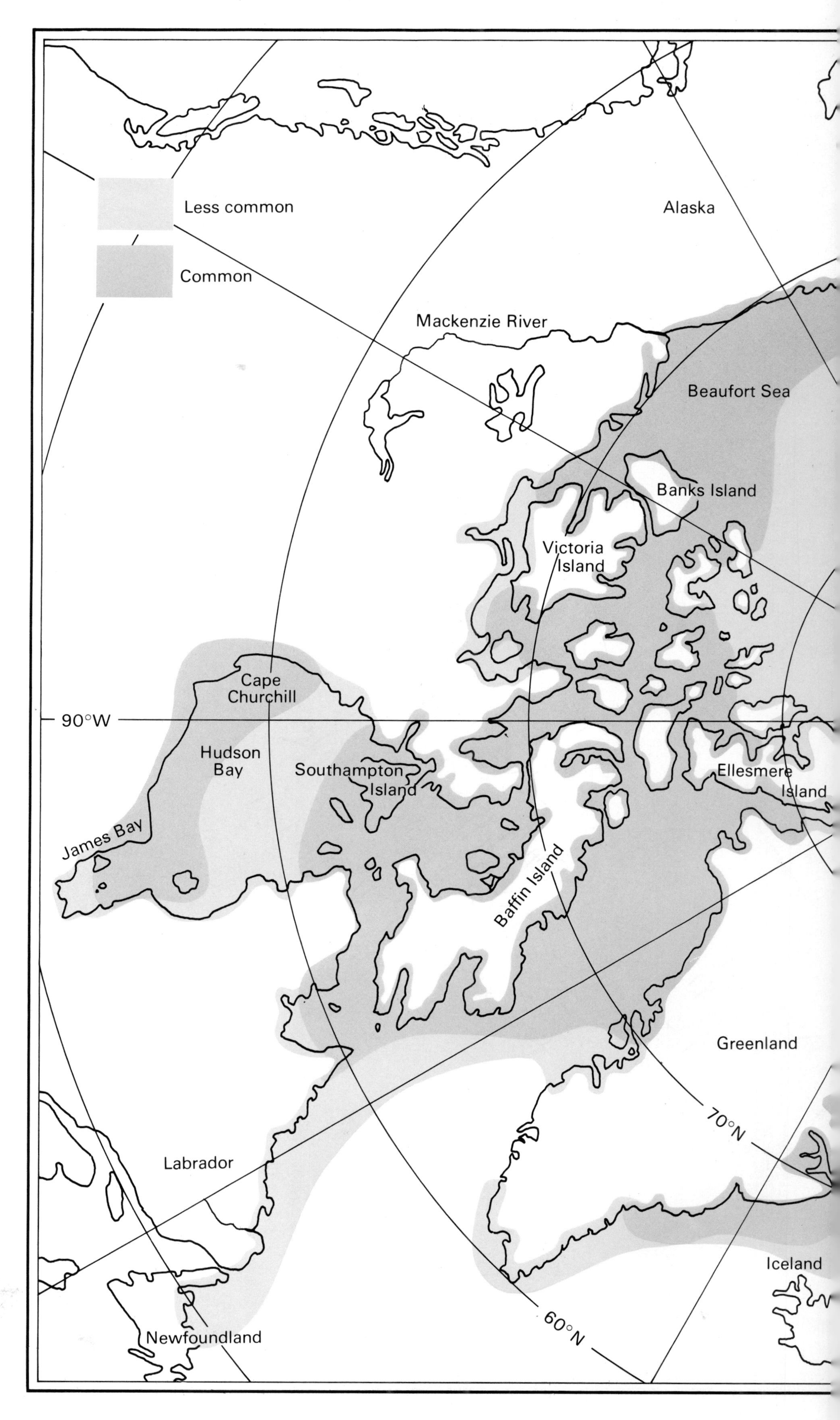

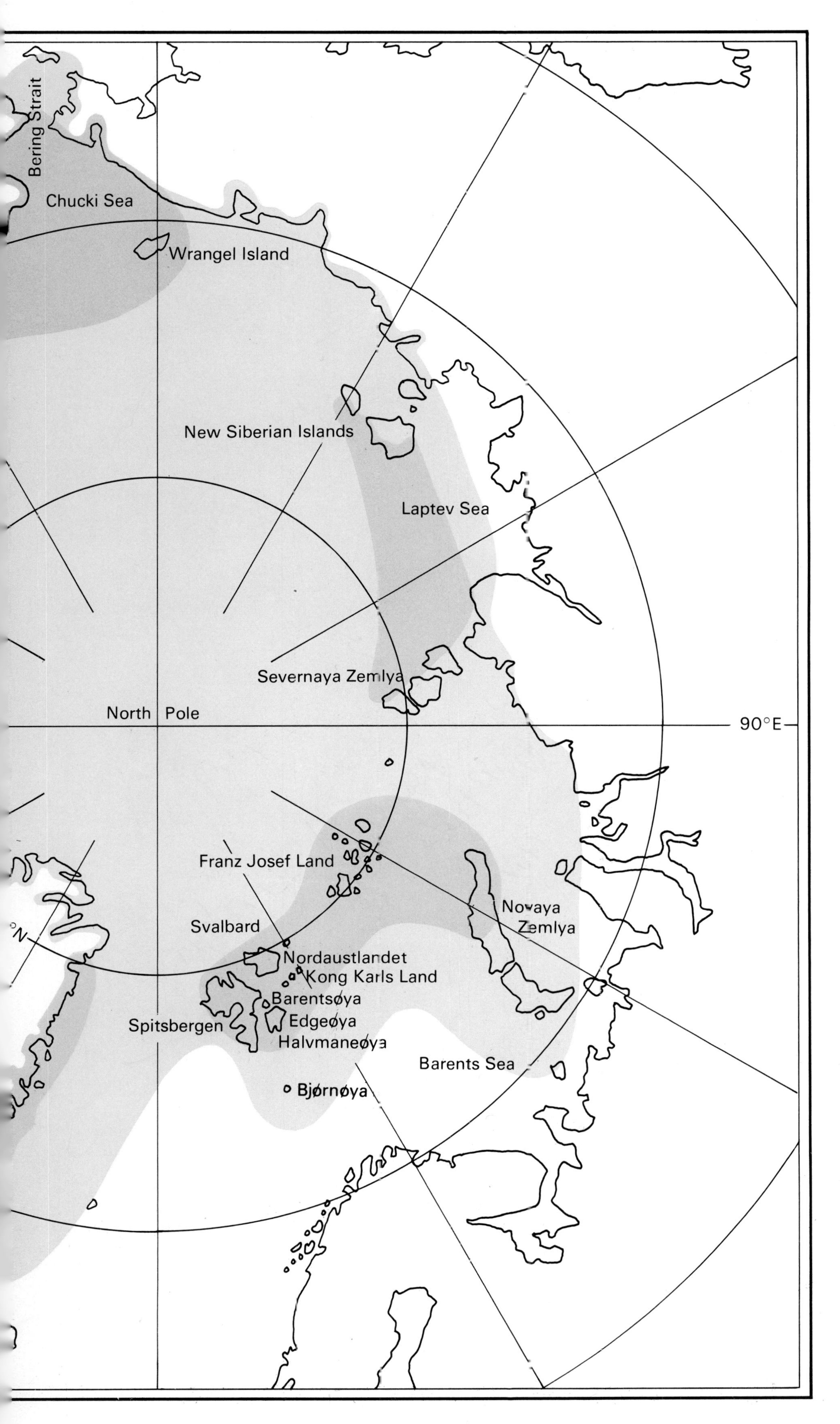
Bering Strait
Chucki Sea
Wrangel Island
New Siberian Islands
Laptev Sea
Severnaya Zemlya
North Pole
90°E
Franz Josef Land
Svalbard
Nordaustlandet
Kong Karls Land
Barentsøya
Edgeøya
Spitsbergen
Halvmaneøya
Novaya
Zemlya
Barents Sea
Bjørnøya

Right
Polar Bears are more carnivorous than other bear species. Their teeth are adapted to eating meat, while other bear species are more herbivorous.

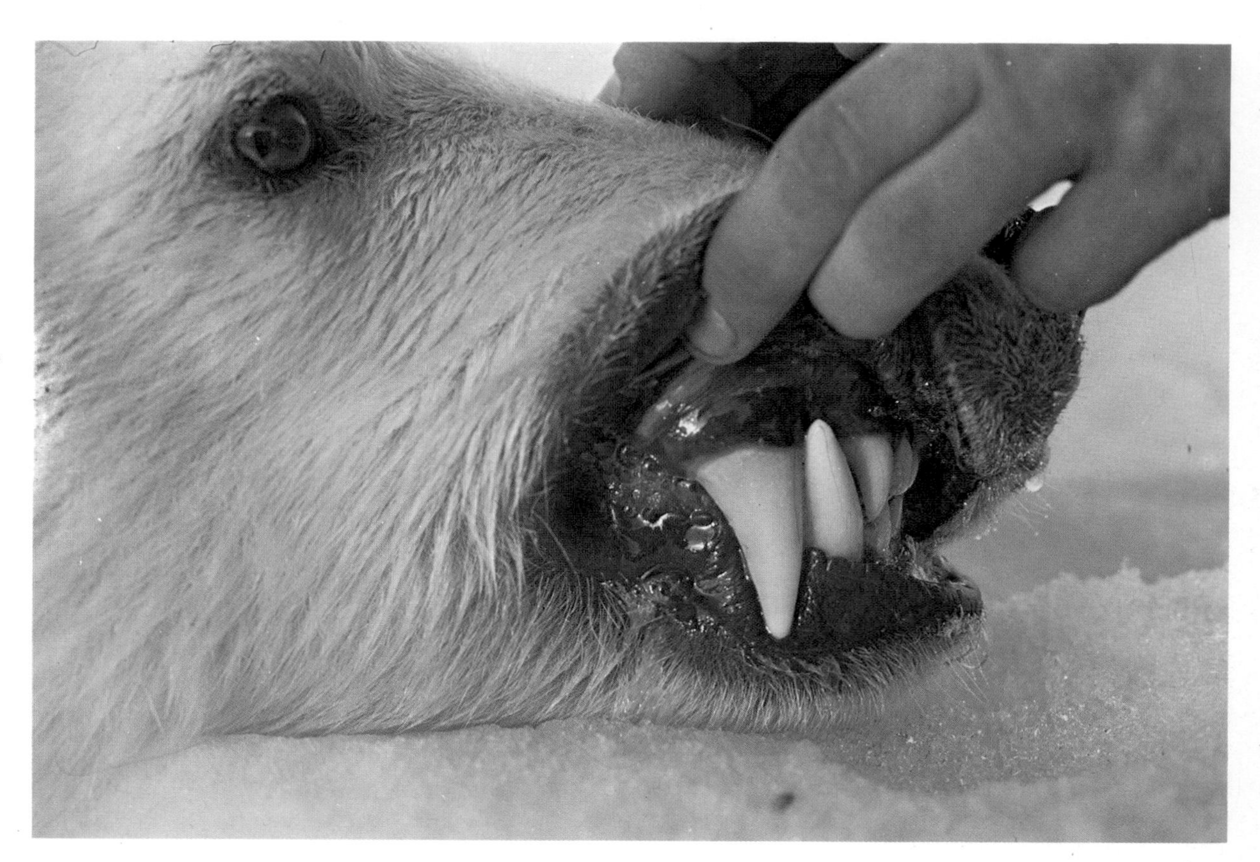

Below right
Polar Bear claws are shorter but also sharper than on other bear species. Brown and Black Bears use their claws for digging. Polar Bear claws are more adapted to holding the prey.

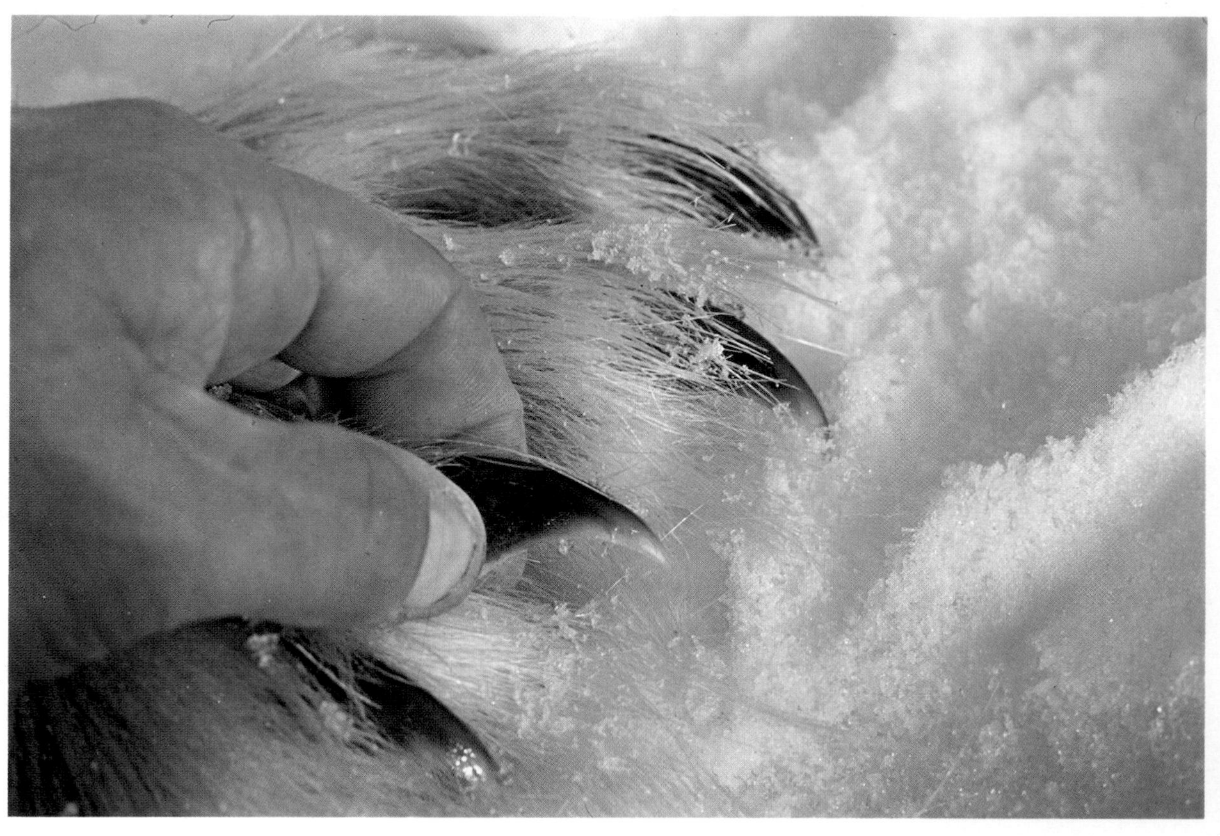

Profiles of Brown and Polar Bears showing the Polar Bear's 'roman nose' and more streamlined profile.

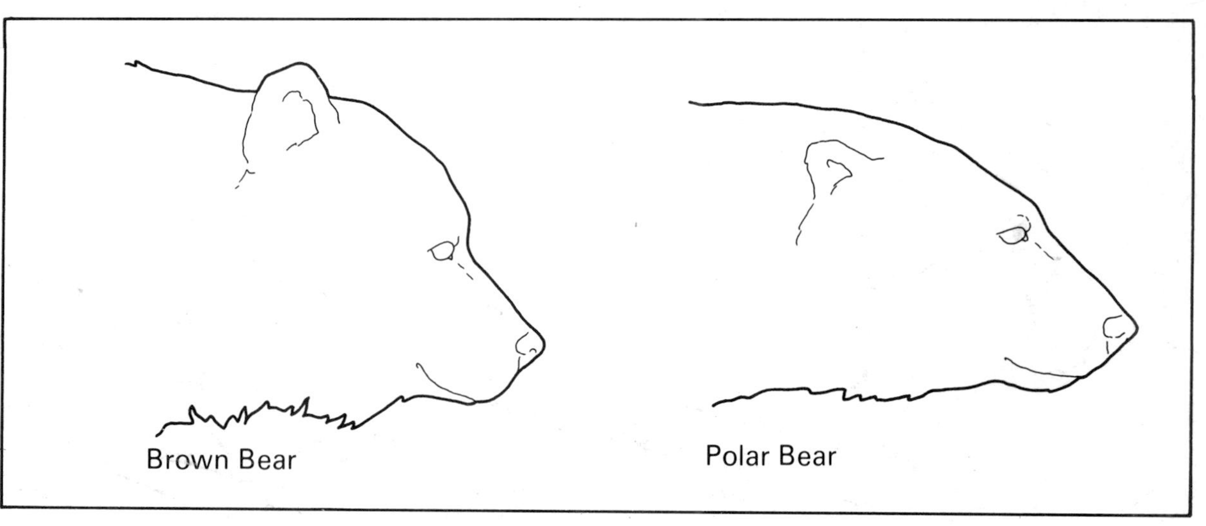

High Arctic. The species is also common along the Alaskan coast, north to about 75°, and south to Bering Strait. Further west, Polar Bears are mainly found around Wrangel Island, in the Laptev Sea between the New Siberian Islands and Severnaya Zemlya, and in the Novaya Zemlya – Frans Josef Land area. They are also abundant in the Svalbard area, in particular in the east and north. Polar Bears are less common in the central north polar basin, where seals are less abundant, although some bears have been observed very close to the Pole.

Above
An aerial view of a Polar Bear crossing a tundra lake at Cape Churchill, Manitoba.

Migration

The Polar Bear depends upon seals for food. The abundance of seals is often determined by ice conditions and the fertility of the polar seas. When ice and food conditions change, the seals will move from one area to another. Some seal species congregate in great numbers when their young are to be born, and also when they mate. Thus Polar Bears will often follow the changing ice in their hunt for seals. They tend to avoid consolidated ice, because there are often few seals present. Where Polar Bears are less abundant in the polar basin, it is mainly because these water masses have a small biological production, and hence few seals. The Danish Polar Bear specialist, Dr. Christian Vibe, claims that Polar Bears are so dependent upon the changes in the ice and the biological productivity in the drift-ice, that these changes would be reflected by an alteration in the Polar Bear catches off Greenland. He has also shown that similar changes occur in the catches of seals, sea birds and fish.

Because alterations in the ice conditions

Left
Polar Bears usually belong to the barren High Arctic coasts and the pack-ice. But in the Hudson Bay in Canada, Polar Bears often move deep into the coniferous forests, where they live much like the Black and Brown Bears.

and the productivity in the polar seas often depend upon the changing seasons, the Polar Bear migratory pattern is often also seasonal. As an example, most bears in the Barents Sea are found on the open drift ice between Svalbard and the western Soviet Arctic islands in summer. Here, there are plenty of Ringed Seals (*Phoca hispida*) and Bearded Seals (*Erignathus barbatus*) among the icefloes. When the ice consolidates and freezes in the autumn, the bears must move to where the seals are, and wander south and west with the ice edge. This was well known among Norwegian Polar Bear trappers, who had their trapping stations often in the middle of these migratory routes, where bears were abundant. On Halvmåneøya (Halfmoon Island) in southeast Svalbard, two trappers could take up to 145 bears in one season. Bears pass this tiny island on their migration west towards the ice edge in the autumn, and on their spring migration eastwards when the ice in the northern Barents Sea breaks up again. In Greenland, Polar Bears are often seen migrating along the frozen fjords in the spring, coinciding with the Ringed Sea pups which are born in dens under the snow on the fjord.

Population discreteness

For many years, scientists, explorers and hunters could not agree whether the Polar Bear belonged to one single population, which constantly was on the move, or several that were more homebound and therefore could be found in the same general area from one year to the next. Some, like the famous Danish explorer and naturalist Alwin Pedersen, were of the opinion that Polar Bears migrated clockwise around the polar basin. Bears which one year were found in Greenland, could cross the Canadian Arctic islands the next, pass the north Alaskan coast and the Siberian coast during the third year, then cross Svalbard (Spitsbergen) and finally head back for the east Greenland coast. Many observers had followed Polar Bear tracks for many miles over pack-ice, pressure ridges and floes, or across fjords and glaciers. For them, too, it was natural to conclude that the Polar Bear was a true vagabond, which one year could be found in one part of the Arctic and another year in quite another region. Others were of a different opinion. They felt that bear migration, occurrence and denning habits were so regular that it was natural to

A Polar Bear female and her yearling on a beach in the Canadian Arctic.

suspect the animals of belonging to stocks with a more or less regular life-pattern. The question of whether we had one or several Polar Bear populations throughout the Arctic has received much attention from scientists, and the problem is still not entirely solved. But markings and recoveries, genetic studies, and comparisons of skull shape and size have shown that there are several, relatively separate populations of bears throughout the Arctic. Most of them are confined to the High Arctic lands and islands and to the adjacent pack-ice areas, where they spend most of their life. Previously it was believed that Polar Bears drifted more or less passively with the drift-ice. We now know that Polar Bears are able to travel against the drift, and are not forced to move helplessly with the currents. Recoveries of marked bears from all parts of the Arctic show that bears tend to stay in the same general area from one year to the next. Comparisons of Polar Bear skulls show that bears in Svalbard and east Greenland are definitely smaller than bears in Alaska and the eastern Soviet Arctic. Scientists now are of the opinion that there is one Polar Bear population in Svalbard, which probably has connections with bears in Frans Josef Land and Novaya Zemlya. The bears on the east Greenland coast probably form one population, which only now and then gets visitors from Svalbard. These bears probably wander across the Greenland Sea, or come across from northwest Greenland along the north Greenland coast. The west Greenland bears probably have connections with bears of the Canadian High Arctic. Canadian scientists are of the opinion that there are perhaps eight or more different populations in the Canadian High Arctic alone. The Canadians also have Polar Bears further south, in the Hudson and James Bays. These bears, which behave and live very differently from the High Arctic Polar Bears, have a diet and ecology more like the Brown Bear. Previously, there were Polar Bears in Labrador, which had specialized in capturing salmon in the rivers, as Brown Bears still do in Alaska. The Labrador Polar Bears are gone now, but their relatives on Twin Islands in the Hudson Bay have also specialized – not in capturing fish, but birds, which are common on the islands. The bears of the Hudson and James Bays also have other denning habits. While bears in the High Arctic regions dig their dens almost exclusively in the snow, these bears often dig their dens partly in soil and gravel. Some dens in the Hudson Bay may be found far inland, in forest areas.

In Alaska, there is probably a northern and a western population, which are relatively separate from each other. The western population probably has connections westwards, across the Bering

Polar Bears along the west coast of the Hudson Bay.

Strait with bears on Soviet territory. Wrangel Island in the eastern Soviet Arctic is a very famous Polar Bear denning area. It is reasonable to assume that many of the Polar Bears which are seen outside the Alaskan coast in winter and early spring actually come from Wrangel Island and the Soviet Arctic. However, documentation is lacking, for it is only recently that the Russians have started marking Polar Bears. In the future, it is hoped more knowledge will be obtained about this common Russian–American Polar Bear population. At the same time, some nations have reduced their yearly 'kill' of bears significantly, and therefore recoveries of marked bears are almost only made through the tagging programs in these countries.

We do not know much about the possible borders of the Polar Bear populations in the Soviet Arctic. But Soviet scientists assume that bears in the Laptev Sea area and adjacent islands are separated from the bear populations in the west and east. Thus there are probably at least three bear populations in the Soviet Arctic.

Some bears undoubtedly wander some distance, across vast pack-ice areas, and migrate from one population to another. Of the more than 360 marked bears which had been recovered by 1974, there were several which had travelled far. One bear, which was marked in Svalbard in 1967, was shot a year later in Nanortalik, in southwest Greenland after wandering more than 3200 kilometres (1984 miles). There are many reports of bears which have been observed on the pack-ice in the central polar basin. Nansen and Johansen, during their efforts to reach the North Pole, met bears on 84° North latitude. The crews on the Arctic Floating Ice Stations have been visited by bears less than 300 kilometres (186 miles) from the North Pole.

Some scientists suggest that there perhaps are separate Polar Bear populations which belong to the polar pack-ice, which breed and den in the pack, and which rarely, if ever, come ashore. We have no reliable information to support this theory, and more research is necessary in order to come to any firm conclusions.

An aerial view of the sea-ice at Nicholson Point in the Canadian Northwest Territories.

Population size

One question which Polar Bear biologists commonly face is: how many bears are there in different parts of the Arctic, and in the northern polar region all together? There are many estimates, but they vary considerably. On the basis of den counts and aerial surveys, Russian scientists in the early 1960s estimated the total world population of Polar Bears at somewhere between 5000 and 8000 animals. At the same time, American biologists suggested that there was a world Polar Bear population of approximately 20 000 animals. Their estimate was based on aerial counts outside the Alaskan coast, and the figures were used as a basis for a world-wide estimate. The Canadians believed that there were about 5000 Polar Bears in Canada alone, and that the world population probably was well over 10 000 animals. Comparative air and ship counts in the Svalbard waters indicated that 1500 to 2000 bears were to be found in that part of the Arctic. Recent estimates by the Russians set the total world population at approximately 15 000 bears.

The estimates are all hampered by inaccurate counting methods, with the probability of overlooking animals, and various other factors affecting the surveys. Although most scientists now agree that the world s total bear population is probably close to 20 000 bears, they also agree that the figures are of little practical importance. It is more meaningful to find out whether the bear population in any given area increases, is stable, or decreases. Information about fluctuations in population sizes come from analysis of 'catch' statistics and data, through marking and recovery of marked animals, through age composition analysis, studies of reproductivity and natural mortality, and through other more indirect research. Also the total number of bears in the world means little as long as the bears belong to separate populations, which have little connection with each other. The important question is therefore: how healthy is each such population, and what seems to be its immediate future? From a conservation standpoint the management aspects are therefore more important than pure knowledge about the population size at a given time.

Young and curious.

Hunting and feeding

Over 90% of the Polar Bear's diet probably consists of seals. The Ringed Seal is by far the most important prey, but Polar Bears also take other species, such as Bearded Seals, Harp Seals (*Pagophilus groenlandicus*) and Hooded Seals (*Cystophora cristata*). The two latter species are mainly preyed upon in their breeding grounds, where seal pups can be found in great numbers, shortly after they have been born in early spring, and when the are still not capable of fleeing into the water.

Polar Bears catch adult seals in many ways. They may stand or lie by a seal's blowhole in the ice for hours – absolutely still and patient, waiting for the seal to surface through the hole to breathe. When this happens, the bear will quickly hit it with its paw, then grab it with its teeth and throw it out of the water and on to the ice. Some naturalists, like the famous Danish explorer Peter Freuchen, claim that the Eskimos must have learned the seal-catching technique from the Polar Bear. Under other conditions bears catch seals by different methods. When the summer ice is broken, and seals are resting on the icefloes, a bear may slip into the water and swim very carefully towards the seal, with only its nose above the water. A short distance from the seal, the bear will dive quietly, swim towards the ice-edge, and then suddenly jump on to the ice and kill the seal. Bears may also take seals by surprise, and sneak upon them while they sleep or sunbath on the ice close to their holes. During such periods, the seals are very alert, and wake up and look around at short intervals. The bear may crawl close, very carefully, trying to hide behind iceblocks and other natural objects. Some trappers claim that the bear hides its nose behind its paw as it approaches the seal. Others find this unlikely, as the paw with its five black claws is just as visible as the nose. Extensive observations of Polar Bear behaviour and hunting methods have recently been made by Dr. Ian Stirling of the Canadian Wildlife Service in the Canadian High Arctic. During more than 600 hours of observations, 288 hunts were observed. No observations were made of a bear using its forepaws to cover its nose. The observations, which were made on old winter ice, revealed that more than 77% of the hunts were still-hunts: that is, bears lying, sitting, or standing at the blowholes waiting for a seal to surface. Almost 23% of the hunts were stalk hunts: that is, bears trying to sneak upon their prey, either on the ice or by the water. When stalk-hunting on the ice, bears would keep low and creep forwards, trying to hide between iceblocks and irregularities on the ice. When at a distance of fifteen to thirty metres (fifty to one hundred feet), the bear would jump-up and race towards the seal in an effort to cut off its escape through the hole. In many cases the attack is too fast for the seal to flee, although it is sleeping right next to the blowhole. The Polar Bear's keen sense of smell is often very important in locating its prey.

In early spring, the Ringed Seal cubs are born in tunnels which are dug out by the mother seals in the snow around the blowholes. These are held open throughout the winter. The blowholes and the tunnels are often covered by one or two metres (three to six feet) of snow and are invisible as the only entrance is from the blowhole, below. Polar Bears can sometimes smell such a seal lair, or 'aglo', and dig out the seal pup. The bear will usually succeed in catching its prey in one out of ten attempts at digging out an 'aglo'. It is nevertheless remarkable that the animal is able to smell its prey through such a depth of snow.

Hunters, naturalists and scientists often discuss how much food a Polar Bear needs per day, and how many seals it will kill in a given situation. The bear's food requirement will vary according to the animal's size and condition, the weather, temperature, wind, the animal's activity, etc.

Opposite above
Harp Seals on the ice.

Opposite below
The Hooded Seal can be a dangerous animal and even Polar Bears tend to avoid them. Pups of this species, however, are often taken by the bears.

Above
The Harp Seal is common in some areas of the Arctic. During the pupping season in early spring, Polar Bears can kill a considerable number of pups, often without eating any of them.

Above right
Caribou and Reindeer are characteristic animals in the Arctic landscape. They often form large herds, which undertake long migrations during the year.

Norwegian sealers can tell that Polar Bears often perform mass kills when they visit the breeding grounds of Harp and Hooded Seals where seal pups are very abundant. Under such conditions, Polar Bears will probably kill an excess number of seals, and only eat the skin and blubber. When there is lack of food, however, and when the bears have gone for long periods without any food, they leave little of their prey. Mr. Nils Øritsland, who has studied Polar Bear physiology and energetics, has estimated that a Polar Bear population of approximately 600 animals in the Hudson Bay area needs a minimum of 8000 seals during an eight month period. A Ringed Seal weighs an average of eighty kilograms (176 pounds), which means that each bear eats at least four kilograms (8·8 pounds) of meat, blubber, skin, bones and intestines each day, as an average.

Canadian and Greenland Eskimos claim that Polar Bears can use tools to hunt the seals. According to them, bears will grab iceblocks or stones which they then smash against the seal's head. Many soapstone and bone carvings from Greenland and the American Arctic show this motif, but trappers from the Norwegian Arctic admit never to having seen such hunting methods. There are, however, observations from zoological gardens which show

BEAR KILLING WALRUS.

that bears are indeed capable of throwing various objects over some distance. But, until recently, documentation of bears using tools to kill seals has been lacking. However, in 1972, a Canadian Wildlife Service group under Mr. Hank Kiliaan, working on Polar Bears in the field in the Grise Fjord area in Arctic Canada, made observations which indicated that a female Polar Bear accompanied by two cubs had broken off an iceblock of approximately twenty kilograms (fifty-four pounds), and probably used it either to break through a Ringed Seal's lair or to smash in the seal's head. Researchers of the Canadian Wildlife Service had noticed, that while they were capturing bears with foot-snares in the Hudson Bay in 1971, some bears were able to spring traps by rolling small rocks on to them.

There are a few reports of Polar Bears taking land mammals. From Svalbard, there are observations of bears and Reindeers (*Rangifer tarandus platyrhynchus*) walking together and even grazing together, while the animals seem to ignore each other. We do know, however, that Polar Bears may occasionally take Muskoxen (*Ovibus moschatus*). A Danish expedition to east Greenland in 1973, found three carcasses of Muskoxen, which had probably been killed by Polar Bears. In

Top
Eskimos in the Canadian Arctic and Greenland claim that Polar Bears can hunt by means of various 'tools'. It is commonly believed that they sometimes crush their prey by throwing an iceblock or stone, but reliable documentation is lacking.

In some regions, large herds of Walruses still gather on the shores, as abundant as they once were in other areas, where man almost exterminated them.

two cases the tracks indicated that the Muskoxen could not get away in deep and loose snow and therefore had been overtaken and killed by the bear.

Most observers claim that Polar Bears are not able to kill Walruses and that they rather fear the species. Some Walruses may develop a partly carnivorous diet. It has been claimed that a Walrus which fights a Polar Bear will try to hold the bear with its powerful foreflippers and then kill it with its tusks. When encountered in the water, a Polar Bear would probably not stand a chance against a Walrus. But there are reports about Polar Bears that have killed Walrus calves, and other, probably romanticized, reports tell of bears which have tried to kill adult animals often by means of iceblocks or stones – but usually in vain.

Polar Bears may also eat seabirds. Canadian scientists have found that Polar Bears on Twin Islands in the Hudson Bay have developed a special technique to dive under flocks of Long-tailed Ducks (*Clangula hyemalis*) and other seabirds and catch them from beneath. We also know that they may take eggs and young

Below
The Kittiwake is common in many Arctic regions. It breeds on steep cliffs, often side by side with Guillemots and other seabirds, and often in colonies which number several thousands.

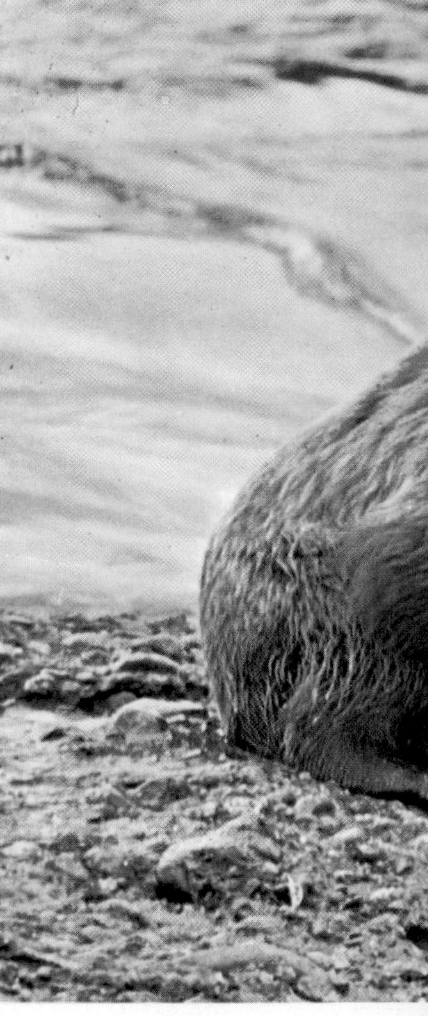

in Eider Duck (*Somateria mollissima*) colonies. Some trappers claim that Polar Bears are excellent climbers and that they may raid steep bird-cliffs with breeding Brünnich's Guillemots (*Uria lomvia*) and Kittiwakes (*Rissa tridactyla*). Canadian scientists have observed Polar Bears stalking and killing adult geese. From Baffin Island, there is a report of a Polar Bear which, after it was killed, was found to have the stomach full of Eider Duck eggs. The raiding of birds' nests and the killing of adult birds seem to be more frequent in some regions than in others. Observations have been made of a Polar Bear which walked through a colony of nesting Snow Geese (*Anser hyperboreus*) without paying any attention to the birds and without disturbing any nests. Examinations of the droppings and stomach contents of bears from several parts of the Arctic show that birds and eggs are not a major food source. In the Hudson Bay in Canada, however, where Polar Bears have adopted their hunting methods to capture birds while they swim on the water, birds, and in particular ducks and geese, make up about 70% of the diet.

Left
While Polar Bears rarely have more than two cubs, three young is relatively frequent in Brown and Grizzly Bears.

Below left
The Barnacle Goose (*Branta leucopsis*) breeds in Greenland, Svalbard and the western Soviet Arctic. The Greenland and Svalbard populations winter in the British Isles.

Brown and Grizzly Bears are famous for their ability to catch salmon migrating upriver in order to spawn. In some Alaskan rivers, like the McNeill River, Brown Bears are often seen in groups, fishing for salmon. More than 200 years ago, when there were Polar Bears in Labrador, they were observed catching salmon. One observation from April 1771 claims that thirty-two Polar Bears were fishing for Atlantic Salmon (*Salmo salar*) in the Eagle River.

In summer, Polar Bears may eat grass, berries, seaweed, and other vegetable material. Both in Svalbard and in Canada, bears have been observed diving for seaweed, which they drag ashore and eat with great pleasure. The study of Polar Bear droppings from the Hudson Bay mainland and from Kong Karls Land in Svalbard during the summer, shows that most of

Above
As the ice breaks up in the Hudson Bay in summer, bears will move ashore and stay there until new ice forms in late autumn.

Opposite top
Many Arctic travellers have had the unpleasant experience of having Polar Bear visits in their camp or cabin. In a short time the bear is able to tear apart almost everything in its search for food.

them contained remnants of vegetation.

Cannibalism does occur among Polar Bears. There are a few observations of single bears which have chased and killed female bears and their cubs, or which have taken cubs which have lost their mothers.

Polar Bears are often frequent visitors to depots and trapper's cabins, where they eat whatever edible matter they can find and often cause considerable damage. The Norwegian explorer Otto Sverdrup writes about such a visit: 'The expedition had had a very peculiar depot master that winter. Strong canvas tents were torn to pieces, tentpoles and other wooden material were smashed and cracked as flatbread, and thrown everywhere. All dogfood was eaten, and much of the provisions for the expedition was also gone.'

In northeast Greenland, a Danish military sledge-patrol '*Sirius*' controls the coast and fjords throughout the year. In winter, they travel by dog-teams over vast areas, often depending upon depots in old trappers' cabins and huts, which are resupplied every summer. During their travels, which may last for weeks and months, the patrol-crew often find their depots visited by bears. The intruders have smashed windows, torn down doors, stoves and chimneys, broken furniture and boxes, and inspected everything possibly edible. The men have found that they must store their provisions in strong, steel ammunition boxes, in order to keep the food safe from the bears. When the frequent damage to huts in northeast Greenland is compared with damage to huts in Svalbard, it is reasonable to suspect that some bears in Greenland have specialized

Below centre
In some areas, as at Fort Churchill in the Canadian Arctic, Polar Bears seek buildings where they can find food. Such nuisance bears can be dangerous, and may cause problems of various sorts.

Below bottom
Many 'garbage-dump bears' stay around dumps for considerable lengths of time. They are often seen seeking out food from burning garbage. If immobilized and transported away, they will often return to the dump after some time.

in this type of robbery. Although many huts are also damaged by bears in Svalbard, it does not occur so often, even though the archipelago has a higher bear density than northeast Greenland.

The forest dwelling Polar Bears in the Hudson Bay, like Brown Bears and Black Bears, often eat roots, grass, berries, rodents, etc. But they also catch seals on the Bay when the sea freezes over. Also in the Hudson Bay some bears have specialized in leftovers from camps and settlements, and are frequent visitors to the garbage dump in Churchill. There have been efforts to immobilize the garbage-dump bears and transport them away from Churchill, but this does not seem to be a permanent solution. After some time, the bears which have adapted to these food sources are back in the dump again.

Mass occurrence at foodsites

Polar Bears are generally solitary animals, which avoid each other except during mating periods or when there occasionally is an abundance of food. Some Eskimo tales refer to occasions when large numbers of bears gathered to feed on whale or Walrus carcasses, which have been stranded or have died from other causes. There are also several stories from Svalbard about such incidents, and some are well documented. In 1852, an expedition from northern Norway killed several hundred Walruses in Svalbard, on Håøya in the southeastern part of the archipelago. The ships were not able to take all the blubber onboard, and the carcasses of an estimated 3–400 animals were left on the beach. The next year captain Kulstad and his crew

Bears along the west coast of the Hudson Bay.

sailed to the islands where the Walrus carcasses had been. In his diary he writes:

'I sent one "catching" boat with harpooner and three men to search the island, to see if any catches could be made. As they came ashore on the island, they met with several Polar Bears, there were about half a hundred of them, which had walked across the ice from the Spitsbergen Island to find food in the big heaps, on the island, Høirox.

A later estimate of the number of bears on the small island was sixty or more. Later in his diary, Kulstad wrote:

'This was my third voyage to Spitsbergen, but my first as harpooner, and even though I have caught many kinds of predatory animal before, I cannot deny that the sight of so many bears set my heart pounding. It was strange to see those clumsy animals, passing each other in different directions around the heaps of carcasses, how they sneezed and growled at each other, and how they turned and threw the big walrus carcasses with the greatest of ease.'

Mating and denning

Polar Bears rarely seek each others company, and are not usually observed together except when peculiar conditions exist; as when, for example, an abundance of food is met with or at a garbage dump or large seal concentration.

From mid-April onwards, female bears are in oestrus and are ready to accept a male. Female bears are normally ready to breed for the first time from four or five years old. They are then approached by the male bears, and as often seen in the animal world, it is the big and strong male which succeeds in courtship, keeping younger and weaker males away. The couple follow each other often for several days and perhaps for weeks. In this period, they may stay together in one general area for long periods. Tracks can be found everywhere, indicating considerable activity on the part of the courting bears. In Greenland we once came upon a big male and a female bear mating in the vicinity of some huge icebergs in Vegasund. The female was accompanied by a two-year-old cub, which respectfully kept at some 100 meters (320 feet) distance after his mother's lover had entered the scene. The two courting animals stayed within a relatively small area. There were tracks everywhere, in circles, zigzags, and back and forth. The tracks showed that they had made long jumps, they had stalked about, and there were marks which showed where they had laid down and rested for some time. Viewed from the air, it was as if there had been a mass congregation of bears in the small area, but the tracks were all from the three animals. The bears were captured and marked. The next year the female was recaptured. Then she was accompanied by two small cubs – thus proving that the mating observed had indeed been a success.

Polar Bears probably have a delayed implantation. This means that the foetus is not developed immediately after mating. The fertilized egg is only developed a few steps and remains at this stage for some months. The same phenomenon has been observed in seals and some other mammalian species. In October or November, when the sea-ice freezes up, the pregnant Polar Bear goes ashore to dig her den. She will find a snowdrift in a hillside, a riverbank, a canyon, or in a place where snow has accumulated sufficiently for her to dig her winter lair. Polar Bear dens differ considerably in their shape and size. Some have long tunnels and are elaborately constructed, with two or more chambers. The chamber in which the cubs are born later in the winter is usually about one metre (three feet) or more in diameter, with roof heights somewhat less. The walls and ceiling are dug out, while the floor is trampled flat and hard under the bear's broad paws. The den opening will soon be closed by drifting snow, and after that a field observer cannot find any signs of the female Polar Bear which rests inside. In there, she is well protected against the biting cold, which sometimes may be well below –40 °C. Strong gales whirl across the mountains and plains, and life conditions are extremely harsh during the Arctic midwinter night, which lasts for more than four months.

Most Polar Bear dens are found along High Arctic shorelines and on island coasts, often less than five kilometres (three miles) inland. In some areas, as on the small island group, Kong Karls Land in Svalbard or on Wrangel Island in the Soviet Arctic, Polar Bear dens are sometimes found only a short distance apart in some hillsides. Sometimes a close examination of the dens after they have been abandoned reveal that two dens are sometimes so close that they could have been taken for one den with two openings. In Wrangel Island, Russian scientists found two Polar Bear dens so close together that there was actually an opening in the wall between them. Although less studied, scientists believe that the Frans Josef Land island group, in the Soviet Arctic,

Opposite top
Most families stay together for about two years. When they have left the mother the young bears may stay together for sometime.

Opposite centre
The Polar Bear female will dig its den in a snowbank in late autumn. The den is opened and abandoned in March or April. An inspection inside will often reveal long tunnels and several chambers.

Opposite bottom
A plan of a Polar Bear den on Kongsøya, Svalbard, discovered in March 1973. Notice the smaller tunnels dug around the main den by the cubs.

also has a very high Polar Bear den density. Other famous denning areas are Banks Island, Southampton Island, Baffin Island, and other islands and peninsulas in the High Arctic. Fewer bears den up in Greenland and along the Alaskan shores. Many bears den as far south as the Hudson and James Bays in Canada.

Bears probably prefer to den on land because there is always a possibility of the ice breaking up and moving, with consequent danger to the dens. Recent investigations have shown that female Polar Bears occasionally make their maternity dens in the winter pack-ice off the Alaskan coast. Here, Polar Bear dens are rare on the mainland, and it seems as if the female bears find the sea-ice to be a more suitable denning habitat.

Usually it is only the pregnant females

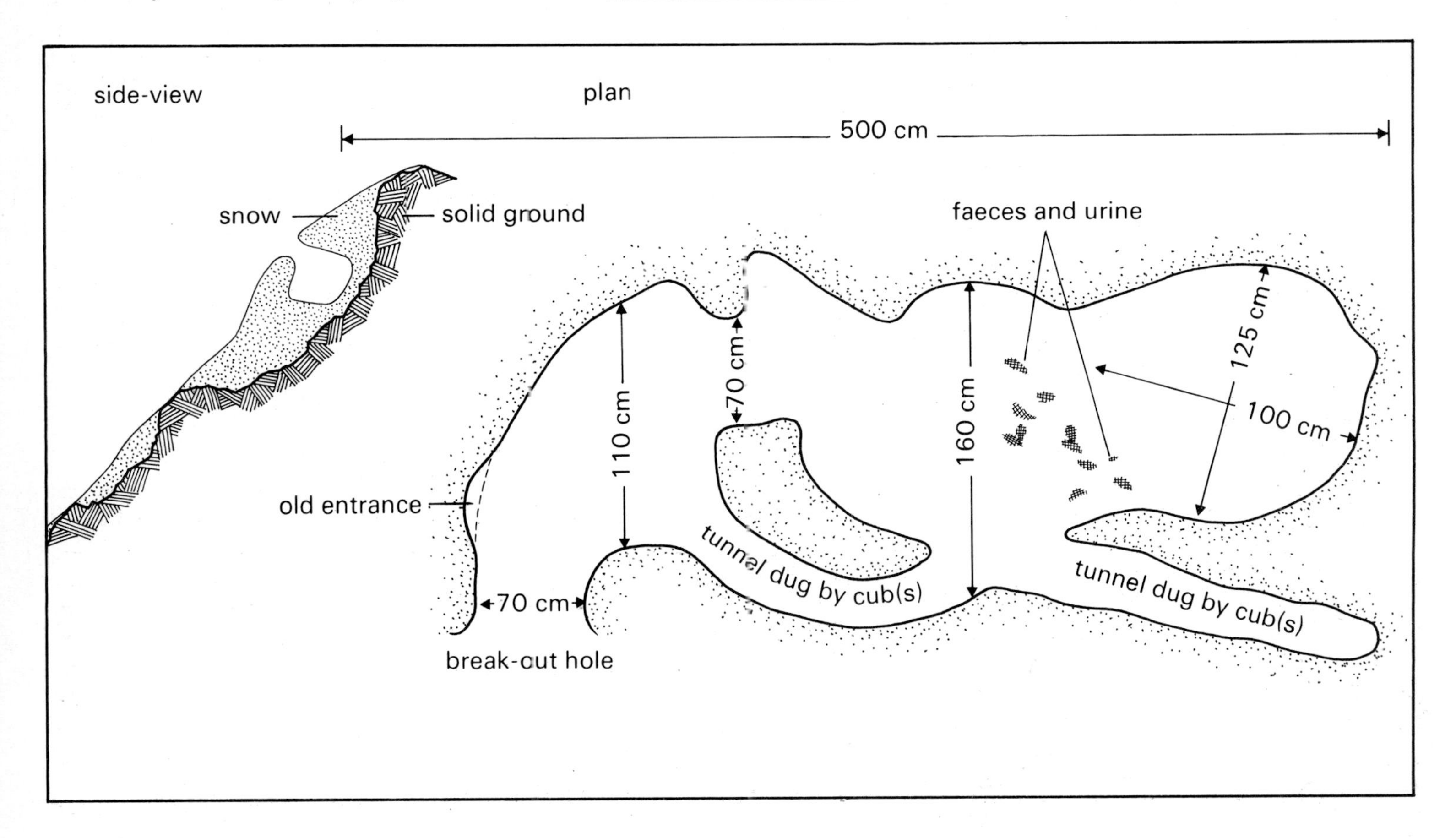

which make dens. But single bears may dig a temporary den where they can stay for some days or a few weeks, because of bad weather conditions or for other reasons.

The Polar Bear is not a true hibernator. The metabolic functions may be somewhat reduced during the denning period, and the animals may become lethargic. They may sleep a lot, but their body temperatures are only slightly below normal. When disturbed in the den, most bears will wake up and start to move about. The cubs are usually born in late December or early January. Usually, there are two cubs in each litter, but there may often be only one. Three cubs in a litter is rather rare. When born, the cubs are very small – not much bigger than a rat – and totally helpless. They are almost naked at birth and blind for about one month. The cubs suckle from their mother in the den, and grow relatively quickly. At two months they weigh about five kilograms (eleven pounds) and move around in the den. Studies have shown that they often dig their own tunnels and small rooms. There has been much discussion as to whether Polar Bears excrete or urinate in their dens. When abandoned, most dens look neat and clean, with only hard trampled snow, and no signs of any droppings. But if the den floor is dug out, it is often revealed that faeces and urine have been covered by snow throughout the winter. When the female bear finds the den too messy from urine and excrements, she probably digs out snow from the roof and walls and tramples it beneath her. When the new floor becomes messy again, the process is repeated. Thus, there may often be several layers of used floors, almost a metre (three feet) thick. If a den is studied after it has been abandoned, one will therefore often find that the construction has

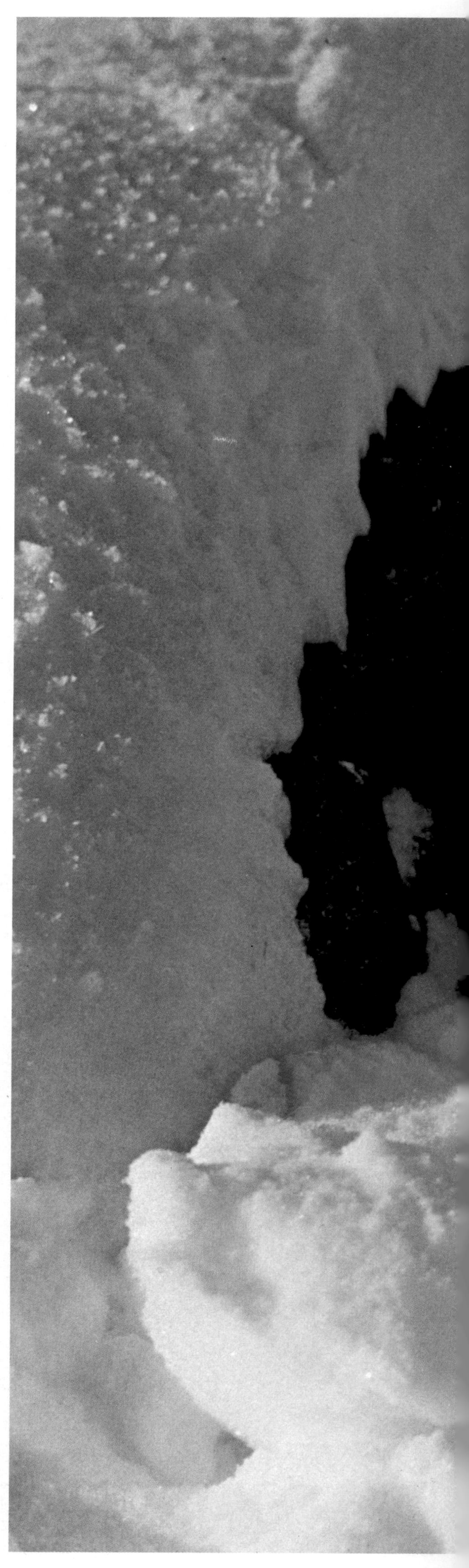

Right
Polar Bear cubs are normally born around Christmas, or a few weeks later. At birth, they are blind, hairless, without teeth and very helpless. When they leave the den about three months later, they are strong and fast. They have a good pelt, and are well prepared for life in the harsh Arctic conditions.

Below
When the Polar Bear cubs leave the den with their mother in March or April, they weigh about ten kilograms (twenty-two pounds), and are about the size of a large dog pup. They are very dependent upon their mother and stay close to her.

This Polar Bear cub is only three months old, but is surprisingly strong and difficult to handle. A firm grasp is required if the man is not to be torn by its very sharp claws and teeth.

been considerably modified since its initial occupation some four months previously.

By mid-March, the cubs have thick fur, weigh about ten kilograms (twenty-two pounds), and are surprisingly strong. A man will have a hard time trying to wrestle a Polar Bear cub at this age. The den is usually opened between mid-March and the first week of April, although some bear families may leave it before, and others may stay in their dens until the first week of May. When opened, many bear families leave their dens immediately, and head for the pack-ice, where the mother bear will hunt for seals. Having stayed in the den without food for more than a few months, the mother bear is often lean. The fat reserves which she accumulated in the autumn are now almost gone, it is therefore understandable that the female now heads for the nearest source of food. Other bear families stay at their dens for a week or more, and seek shelter there whenever bad weather breaks out or any danger threatens the cubs.

The Polar Bear cubs usually follow their mother for two and a half years. In the beginning, they are very dependent upon the mother and when endangered they usually keep close to her, whether they are running or swimming in the sea. The bear family tries to avoid outsiders; single bears may try to chase and kill the cubs if there is an opportunity. Dr. Stirling's observations from the Canadian High Arctic have shown, however, that adult male bears, which are bigger than the females, do not always dominate females with cubs. Also many observations show that smaller bears in most cases will flee when encountering a Polar Bear family group.

The Polar Bear cubs suckle from their mother for many months, and occasionally for more than a year. But they will also soon learn to catch seals for themselves, although with limited success initially. Observations have also shown that eighteen-month-old cubs behave almost like adult bears during their seal hunts, but they lack the patience and skill of the older bears. Observations have been made of thirty-month-old cubs catching seals but still with their mothers. If the mother bear is killed during the first eighteen months, the cubs will most likely die from hunger, be killed by other bears or die from other causes. Cubs will usually stay with their mother's body for a long time, often for days. Thus, when the set-gun was still permitted, it often happened that cubs or yearlings were killed by passing bears after the mother had been killed. For many years, scientists and others have discussed whether female Polar Bears adopt cubs which have been orphaned. This phenomena had been observed in Black and Brown Bears, but not in Polar Bears until recently. In 1973, however, we captured a Polar Bear female with two small cubs in northeast Greenland. The next year, in 1974, we were there again and, among other bears, recaptured this family. But this time the mother bear had four yearlings. She had adopted two others in addition to her own. Dr. Vibe found that this might have happened just before she was recaptured. In the same region, a sledge patrol had found a carcass of a female Polar Bear – probably the mother of two yearlings – just prior to Dr. Vibe's capture of the large family group. The dead female had been killed by another bear, but her offspring had been able to get away. The scientists assumed that the marked female bear had adopted the two motherless yearlings shortly after the loss of their mother. Observations showed that she was able to look after all four.

Summer pack-ice and typical Polar Bear habitat. Here, seals can be found swimming in the leads, or basking in the sun on the ice, and seabirds can be seen everywhere.

Right
Polar Bear cubs do not leave their mother after she has been killed. Pitiful scenes like this have been experienced by most Arctic hunters and trappers.

Below
Mother bear with two six-month-old cubs in the summer pack-ice.

Natural mortality factors

Polar Bears have few enemies. However, as previously mentioned, bears do occasionally kill each other. There are reports of Walruses that have killed bears, and other reports which claim that Polar Bears in certain regions are able to prey upon Walrus females and calves. Observations from the Canadian Arctic show that Polar Bears which follow leads and ice-edges in search for food tend to avoid Walruses which may rest on the ice. There are several, more or less reliable, reports of bears which have been attacked and killed by Walruses in the water. Although the Walrus is a huge, clumsy animal on land, it moves fast and with ease in the water. The Polar Bear, on the other hand, is a relatively slow swimmer. We also know that Polar Bears avoid the male Hooded Seals, which are strong and fast and probably able to give a small- or medium-sized Polar Bear a tough fight.

But there are other dangers which take their toll. Although the Polar Bear is a tough swimmer, many probably drown either because they are hurt in pressure ridges or between floes, or sometimes because large areas of ice with bears on drift away out in the open sea. Occasionally bears come ashore in Iceland, when the ice edge is unusually far south, as it was in 1968. Bears also come ashore on the Norwegian coast. These must be animals which have come from the Barents Sea, on icefloes or by swimming. There are also reports of bears which have come south through the Bering Strait to Japan. Many of these animals are extremely lean, undernourished, and exhausted. We can expect that many others must have perished in the open sea before they came ashore.

Because Polar Bears usually avoid each other, they rarely get involved in fights. When bears occasionally meet on the ice or on the tundra, they will pass each other at distances of fifty to one hundred metres (164 to 328 feet) or more. In the mating season, however, in early spring, males may fight and sometimes hurt each other badly, although deaths are probably infrequent.

Above
The Walrus is probably the only Arctic animal which the Polar Bear respects. Although it has been claimed that Polar Bears can kill Walruses, most observations indicate that they keep a good distance. There are also several reports of bears which have been killed by Walruses.

It has been speculated that cannibalism may serve to regulate the population size when bears become too abundant in a given area and a possible food supply becomes short.

Cubs and young bears are probably rather vulnerable and may have a higher death rate than older bears. We know that newborn cubs are very helpless, and although they are well protected in their dens and although their mothers take good care of them, we know that some of them die in the den. Histological investigations of the female Polar Bear's reproductive organs have shown that she may give birth to an average of more than two cubs. But

Above top
Scientists believe that many bears die on the open sea, when they drift off on an icefloe, and cannot get back to the shore or the pack-ice. Although they are strong swimmers, they are not able to catch food in open water, and will eventually perish.

Above
A Polar Bear family group on an icefloe in the northern Barents Sea.

when the mother bear and her cubs leave the den, she has an average litter size of about 1·7 cubs. The data – although scant – indicates that some cubs die during or shortly after birth. Outside the den, life conditions are harsh, and the small ones may sometimes die under circumstances where an adult bear may survive.

Dr. Christian Vibe observed a female bear with two cubs which were crossing an area with newly frozen sea-ice. The family group dived under the sea-ice, and at certain intervals, the mother bear broke through the ice in order to breathe. The small cubs had evidently great difficulties in swimming under the ice. First one cub disappeared before it reached an opening. Soon afterwards, the second cub also drowned under the ice.

Polar Bear young are also vulnerable when they are abandoned by their mothers after two years or more. From then on they have to tackle all the difficulties and dangers alone. Although little information exists, it is likely that quite a few subadult bears perish in this period. Young bears are generally more curious than older animals which have experienced a lot of dangers during their life. They are more likely to approach ships, humans, trapping devices, etc. – a move which in many cases has a fatal consequence for them.

Above
The physiologist Nils Øritsland with a four-month-old bear cub. Nils put a lot of effort into taming this cub for later research.

Below
Polar Bears often get overheated when forced to run for some time. Therefore the need to cool off and get rid of excess body heat is probably a major reason for fleeing to open water.

Avalanches and snowslides may kill Polar Bears when they are in their dens during winter and early spring. On Kong Karls Land, carcasses and remnants of Polar Bears have been found at the foot of mountain sides and steep hills. Some of those bears have undoubtedly been killed by avalanches. On the same small archipelago, which at times of the year has a very high Polar Bear density, several carcasses and skulls have been collected over the decades, from bears which have died a natural death. The remnants are from bears of all age groups, therefore indicating that natural deaths can occur at all age levels.

Research and conservation

Opposite top
This simple trap is very effective for catching Arctic Foxes. The bait is mounted on the stick underneath the trap-door. When the fox takes the bait, the three sticks mounted in a figure '4' fall apart, and the animal is killed.

Opposite centre
A foot-snare for Polar Bears. The snare is placed in the middle of the trap and anchored to a heavy log. The bait is placed behind the snare, when the bear moves in, it will put its paw down between the sticks and trigger-off the snare.

Opposite below
The set-gun was an effective but also much criticized hunting device for Polar Bears. It is now prohibited, but the boxes where the rifles were mounted and old bear skeletons still tell their story.

Because Polar Bears live in one of the most remote areas of the world, which was once almost inaccesible to man, little was previously known about the biology of this big carnivore. Data and information which has been presented in the previous chapters is mainly the result of Polar Bear research in recent years. Only a few decades ago, theories about the life history and biology of the Polar Bear were often contradictory. Crucial information which was necessary for the management and conservation of the species was lacking, such as data on population status, hunting pressure, reproductive capacity and natural mortality. Systematic research on Polar Bears had not been made, except for some studies on animals in zoological gardens. But as human activities increased in the Arctic, the need for proper management and protective measures became more and more urgent. Strong ships were able to penetrate the pack-ice. Aircraft crossed the Arctic regularly. Snow-machines travelled almost everywhere. On top of this new and modern weapons made the Polar Bear an easy match for any hunter. There was an evident need for more information on the life history and biology of the Polar Bear in order to meet the problems which were created by the increasing human activity.

In 1965, the United States of America invited representatives from Canada, Denmark, Norway and the USSR to participate in The First International Scientific Conference on the Polar Bear in Fairbanks, Alaska. The meeting was held 'to permit scientists and conservationists from interested Arctic nations to meet to discuss the future of the magnificent Polar Bear which inhabits the Arctic Polar Basin and roams at will without regard to national boundaries'. Here biologists and decision-makers from the five circumpolar nations who were concerned with the protection of Arctic fauna and flora presented their national research efforts and hunting control measures. The participants discussed immediate and long term measures which were required to protect the Polar Bear from depletion of its numbers, as well as the necessity of exchanging data, and the coordination of efforts on an international basis. One of the major objectives of the conference was '. . . the establishment of a machinery to gather, evaluate and distribute information for the future'.

At that time, the Polar Bear hunt in Canada was mainly performed by the northern native people. But there were few restrictions to hunting methods and means. Most Canadian Eskimos used dog-teams and snow-machines on their Polar Bear hunts. The annual 'kill' was around 600 bears and hunters took single bears as well as females with cubs and yearlings. The Polar Bears were hunted by the Eskimos mainly for the value of the pelt. Some pelts were used by Eskimo families for trousers and other personal necessities, while the rest were sold to tanners and fur-trade companies. The Canadian Wildlife Service had initiated a Polar Bear study program in 1961, which aimed to review the effectiveness of protective measures and legislation. The research by this institution included taxonomic studies, den studies, research on reproductivity in the bears and various other problems. This research was to continue and there was to be an increase in their efforts in research fields which were related to conservation and management.

In Greenland, only residents were permitted to hunt Polar Bears. This meant that natives, and also Danes who had lived more than two years in Greenland, were permitted to hunt. Most bears were taken by the Eskimos using the traditional dog-sledge. There were few hunting regulations in force, however, in northeast Greenland, Polar Bear cubs and females with cubs were protected: bears could only be hunted between November 1 and May 31; the use of poison, foot-traps, set-guns and aircraft was prohibited; guns had to be 6·5 mm. calibre or more. About a hundred bears were killed in Greenland annually. Apart from Alwin Pedersen's work, Dr. Christian Vibe had studied the relationship between climatic fluctuations and animal abundance in Greenland. The Zoological Museum in Copenhagen collected Polar Bear skulls whenever possible.

In the Norwegian Arctic, Polar Bears were mainly hunted by sealers in the pack-ice off east Greenland (the 'West Ice') and in the northern Barents Sea (the 'North Ice') and other ice areas. Many bears were also taken by wintering trappers and by the crews on the weather stations in Svalbard. The average annual Norwegian catch in the postwar years was more than 300 bears. There had been a gradual shift in the hunting effort, as fewer ships hunted bears, the wintering trappers and weather-station crews took increasingly more bears. From 1952, the tourist Polar Bear hunt began to develop in Svalbard. Tourist hunters could participate in a ten day cruise with a sealing vessel to the Barents Sea pack-ice, where they were permitted to shoot one bear each. There were few Norwegian regulations governing the Polar Bear hunt. The bears have been protected on Kong Karls Land – a tiny island group in the eastern Svalbard waters – since 1939. The taking of cubs was prohibited and required special permission. Certain killing methods such as the use of poison, and foot-traps were prohibited. But the traditional set-gun was still permitted and accounted for the majority of the take in Svalbard. The set-gun (Norwegian: Selvskudd) consists of a wooden box on four poles, about seventy-five centimetres (thirty inches) above the ground. A rifle or a shotgun was mounted in the box, and a bait placed in front of the muzzle. A string was fastened to the bait, and when a Polar Bear grabbed the bait with the teeth, it would trigger the gun.

Left
Scientists also capture Polar Bears by the use of foot-snares, so that they can be immobilized afterwards. Such devices never harm the animals. After a short fight, the bear gives up and lays down until the scientist comes along with his syringe-gun.

Travelling by dog sledge in the Arctic is a unique and unforgettable experience. Snowmachines may be faster, but they are also noisy and do not allow you to enjoy your surroundings in the same way as the traditional mode of travel.

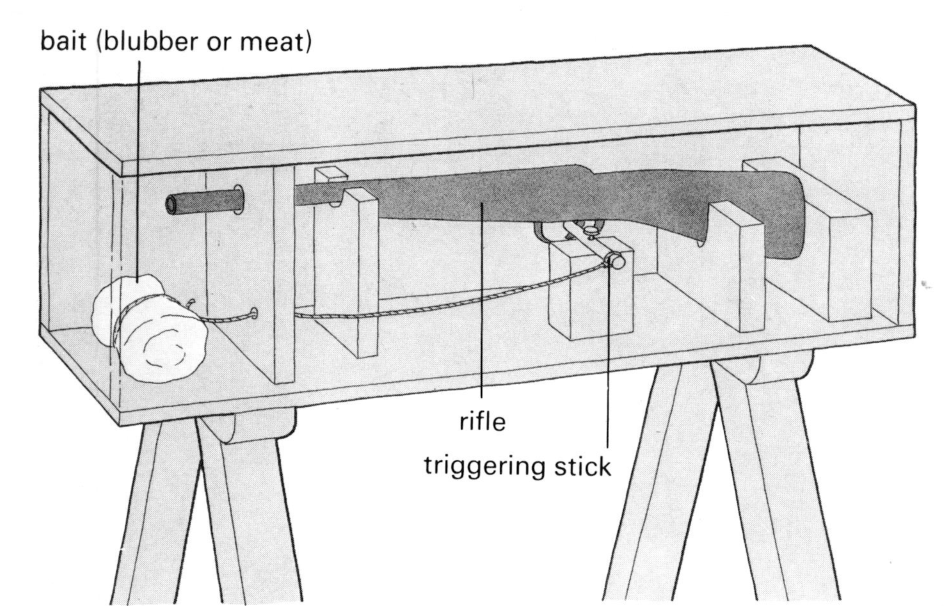

A set-gun mechanism. When the bear pulls on the bait, the attached string pulls the triggering stick around the nail and so fires the rifle.

The set-gun was very effective if properly mounted. Two trappers could take 145 bears in one season on Halvmåneøya, most of them by the use of set-guns. But if built and mounted by an inexperienced person, the set-gun could wound several bears. Another disadvantage of this method was that, obviously, it did not distinguish between single bears and females with cubs. Thus, probably the most valuable elements of the population were often killed. It was also possible for the set-gun to kill the mother bear and leave the cubs behind, who then became an easy prey for single bears.

Norwegian research on Polar Bears until the Conference had been only spasmodic. Some statistics on the 'catch' had been collected by the Directorate of Fisheries. Dr. Odd Lønø had performed some studies during his winter expeditions in Svalbard. A Polar Bear study program, consisting of an ecological and a physiological project, had just been launched by the University of Oslo and the Norwegian Polar Institute.

In Alaska, most Polar Bears were killed by the Eskimos up to about 1950. They used Polar-Bear furs for personal clothing etc., but some hides were also sold. The hunting of Polar Bears by non-resident hunters, who used aircraft, began in the late 1940s. Gradually, there was an almost total shift from the traditional Eskimo Polar Bear hunt to the trophy hunt and sport hunt from aircraft. This hunting method involved the use of two light, ski-equipped fixed-wing aircraft. They worked together for safety reasons. Normally, each plane would carry a guide and a hunter. The guides searched the pack-ice outside Kotzebue, Teller, Point Hope, and Barrow. When they picked up a track which looked fresh, they followed it until the bear was found. One aircraft with a hunter would then land, and the other would keep in the air and perhaps herd the bear towards the hunter. After the kill, the bear was skinned, and the hide was flown back to the base. Hunters paid considerable guide and pilot fees for such hunts, and a bear hide could cost them more than $3000. But there were strong public feelings against the Polar Bear trophy hunting. By 1965 the annual Polar Bear 'take' in Alaska was close to 300 bears. Before 1948 Alaska did not have any significant regulations for Polar Bear hunting. Bag limits were introduced in 1955, and females with cubs and the cubs themselves were protected by the late 1950s. Closed seasons came in 1960, and, during the following year, it was required that Polar Bear hides were tagged. Through the Alaska Department of Fish and Game, the USA established a research program on Polar Bears, related to the management of the species. Biological samples were collected from hunters. Guides and hunters reported on bears observed. Size of hides, skulls, the sex of killed bears and other data were recorded.

In the Soviet Union, Polar Bears had been protected since 1956. Under special permission, cubs could however be taken

Known Polar Bear hunting in Arctic countries

Year	Canada	USA	Denmark	Norway	USSR
1965	565	296	182	435	—[2]
1966	603	399	116	185	—
1967	710	191	150	263	—
1968	454	351	153	267	—
1969	407	298		346	—
1970	323	316		515	—
1971	416	203		116[1]	—
1972	501			61[1]	—
1973	523	7[1]		41[1]	—
1974	583	40–50[1]		—[2]	—
1975				—[2]	—
1976				—[2]	—

[1] Restrictive regulations reduce the annual hunt
[2] Polar Bear hunting prohibited

An aerial view of a dog sledge being driven through the Canadian Northwest Territories.

for zoological gardens. The Central Game and Parks Department and Moscow State University began Polar Bear studies in the mid-1950s. Several expeditions were arranged, in particular to the important Polar Bear denning areas on Wrangel Island. After 1965, the coordination of Soviet Polar Bear research was handled by the USSR Ministry of Agriculture. Work was concentrated on population censuses and population dynamics, denning surveys, in particular on Wrangel Island and Frans Josef Land, and aerial surveys over large areas of pack-ice off the Soviet Arctic coast.

The First International Scientific Conference discussions made it evident that much more information was needed in order to carry out proper national and international management of the Polar Bear throughout the Arctic. In the Soviet Union the problems were not so urgent, because of the total protection enforced. But in all countries, human activities in the Arctic were increasing, and new technical devices made it possible for man to work in the most remote parts of the Arctic, where Polar Bears previously had no competitors for space, and where nothing disturbed their way of living.

The scientists agreed that it was necessary to pay special attention to certain problems, where information was particularly scarce. Such topics were: population discreteness; the relative and absolute numbers of bears throughout the Arctic; migratory patterns; studies of denning biology and reproduction; mortality factors and food biology. These aspects of research could reveal knowledge which would be

Drift ice in the northern Barents Sea. The ice will consolidate and open with the changing wind and currents. The relatively shallow Barents Sea is rather productive, and has a good Polar Bear population.

crucial for a proper management and conservation. The validity of the theory about a uniform circumpolar migrating Polar Bear population was much discussed. This theory which had been launched by many scientists and naturalists, including the Danish scientist A. Pedersen, got considerable support from the Russians, but was questioned by the other delegates. The validity of the theory would naturally have serious management implications. If Pedersen and his supporters were right, conservation and hunting regulations on Polar Bears would almost exclusively be an international problem. But if there were several discrete populations, such steps would rather involve national or bilateral considerations.

The Conference recommended that the International Union for the Conservation of Nature (IUCN) should serve as a clearing house for future collaboration and exchange of information on the Polar Bear. Under its Survival Service Commission, the IUCN had already established several Specialist Groups, which served as advisory organs to governmental and intergovernmental agencies. The IUCN, which was often characterized as the International Red Cross organization for nature conservation, had consultative status to several United Nations organizations, and had good ties with governments in most countries. IUCN had also very close ties with its sister organization the World Wildlife Fund (WWF). The two have a common headquarters in Morges, Switzerland. The WWF is another international organization concerned with nature conservation, but the WWF's major task is to collect funds for the various conservation projects around the world.

The conference agreed that in order to obtain data and samples, effective live capturing methods had to be worked out. The first effort to capture Polar Bears for marking and studies had already been made in March and April of 1965. The Arctic Institute of North America sponsored a pilot study, where biologists searched the pack-ice with fixed-wing aircraft for Polar Bears in the same manner as the trophy hunters. I had been invited to participate in this study by Dr. Martin W. Schein from the University of Pennsylvania. We worked out from the Arctic Research Laboratory at Barrow, Alaska. When a bear was spotted, we tried to land and shoot it with a syringe gun and immobilizing drugs. However, the syringe gun is only effective at distances under thirty to forty metres (100 to 130 feet), while a modern rifle can kill a bear at ten times that distance. Only in one case did we get close enough to shoot a syringe in the bear. But the drug did not take effect, and the bear ran away. It was assumed that better results could be obtained by the combined use of a fixed-wing aircraft and a helicopter. Bears could also be immobilized from icegoing vessels in the summer pack-ice, or be captured by use of foot-

traps, which already had proved successful on other bear species in North America.

During 1966 new initiatives were taken in capturing, handling and marking Polar Bears. Dr. Charles Jonkel of the Canadian Wildlife Service centred his work around the Cape Churchill area, where he and his crew captured four bears by the use of foot-snares. When restrained in this way, bears could be immobilized with drugs delivered with a syringe gun. The same summer, two North American Polar Bear specialists, Dr. Albert W. Erickson of the University of Minnesota and Dr. Vagn Flyger of the University of Maryland and myself, tried to capture bears east of Svalbard. The animals were chased in the pack-ice with an icegoing vessel and were then immobilized by means of the syringe gun. This 'hunt' followed the pattern used by trophy hunters in these waters. When swimming in the sea just below the stern, the bear could not get away, and was an easy target for the man with the syringe gun.

During the following years the Polar Bear research programs expanded considerably in all five Arctic countries. In Canada, the Canadian Wildlife Service performed aerial surveys as well as continuing their trapping efforts in the Hudson Bay area. Telemetry techniques were introduced: small radio transmitters were made into collars which were fastened around the bear's neck. This caused problems, because the Polar Bear's head is not much bigger than its strong and muscular neck, and it is also almost bottle-shaped. Thus transmitters could only be fastened to fully grown animals, and even in those cases, not too tight. The result was often that the bears managed to tear the collar off. Nevertheless, the scientists were able to track some bears, and map their movements. In Svalbard, Norwegian scientists initiated an aerial survey program between March and October, over the Barents Sea pack-ice and the known denning areas. Live capturing, marking and other studies were repeated from a vessel in the summer pack-ice. This time the ship had a small laboratory on board and a strong cage on deck, where bears were kept until they were completely recovered from the immobilization. Fifty-one bears were successfully captured and marked during July and August. Blood, teeth, and various measurements were taken, and each bear was marked with eartags, and a tattoo; a number was also dyed into the fur. Physiological investigations were made on some bears. These studies aimed at a better understanding of the bear's thermoregulation How could this animal swim for hours in ice-cold water or live through winters with extreme cold and blizzards, without freezing to death? How could he manage warm, calm and sunny days during summers without having great difficulties with excess heat? Apart from this study program, Norwegian researchers also collected 'catch' data and biological

Scientists often capture swimming cubs using an aluminium ring mounted on a pole, and then immobilize them by means of a hand syringe.

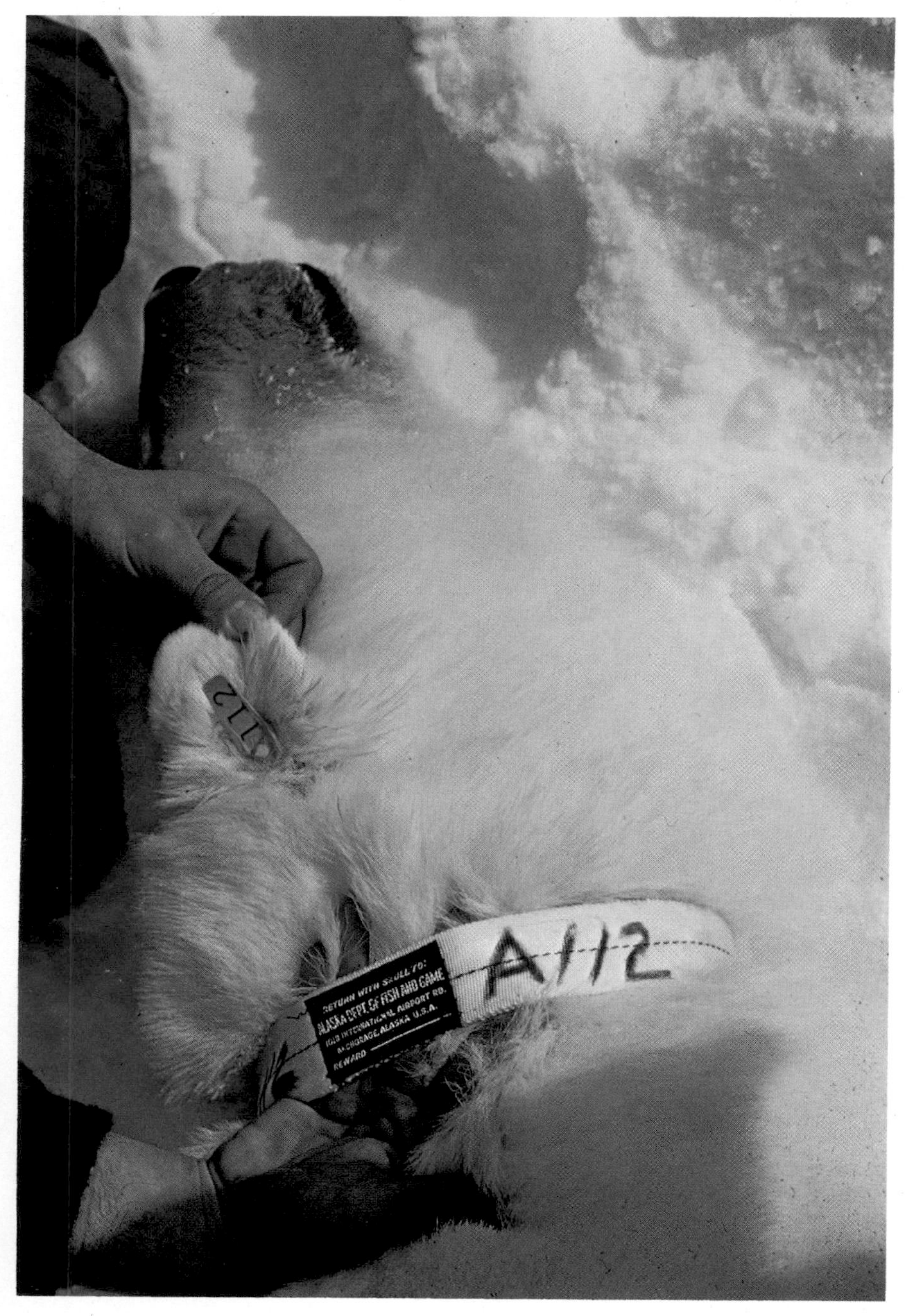

samples from trappers and weather-station crews.

The following pages describe in more detail what actually happens during a Polar Bear field-expedition including its planning and preparation. Firstly, the originators of the project have to consider the scientific as well as the logistic aspects of the expedition. At this stage, discussions with colleagues and studies of the literature give an increasing understanding of the problems and priorities, which are essential in the outlining of the scientific program. However, because it is difficult to predict ice and weather conditions, bear abundance, efficiency of sampling methods etc., alternative approaches must be worked out. There is so much investment in a Polar Bear field research expedition that bad planning cannot be tolerated. Funding is always a problem. Because of the high cost incurred in renting helicopters or chartering ships, as well as the expense of field equipment such as snow machines, an expedition of this nature is always costly. Some nations sponsor such research through federal budgets. But in other cases, the launching of Polar Bear field research programs depends upon sources from various national and international funds. Then, the competition is often high, and Polar Bear research is weighed against other, often very different projects, not only in biology but in other fields of science as well. Often Polar Bear research takes second place to other more urgent projects. Nevertheless, there is an increasing interest and understanding of the need for studies into Arctic biology and ecology.

Polar Bear research takes place in

Above
Scientists have tested various marking techniques during their research programs. A collar fastened around the bear's neck offers possibilities for visual identification, without capturing the bear.

Right
Researcher handling an immobilized female Polar Bear with two cubs, in East Greenland. The family was recaptured one year later. Then the mother had adopted two orphaned cubs, and had a litter of four (see page 53).

remote areas, where resupplying during the expedition period may be difficult or even impossible. Thus nothing must be forgotten when the actual field research begins. But even when we are convinced that every detail has been considered, things may still have been overlooked and confusions may occur.

For example, once, we faced a difficult situation, which required some fast thinking. We were sitting in Longyearbyen in Svalbard late one night preparing for a field trip and packing our equipment. Tents and other field equipment, provisions, sampling and laboratory equipment, phials, eartags, syringe gun, drugs – everything seemed to be there. Vagn Flyger was checking the immobilizing equipment when he suddenly looked up. 'The charges,' he said, 'they are missing!'

The charge is a very essential part of the syringe-gun equipment. It is a small explosive capsule which is put behind the rubber plunger, inside the syringe projectile. When the gun is fired and the flying syringe hits an animal, the charge goes off and pushes the plunger forwards. Without the charge, the plunger cannot move and the syringe cannot be emptied of its immobilizing drug. Therefore, the equipment was practically useless – unless we invented a substitute. The expedition vessel would sail in only a few hours, and new charges could not be obtained before we left. 'We must do something,' Vagn exclaimed. So everybody sat down at the table with the empty syringe in front of us. Several solutions were presented. There were many more or less realistic suggestions which were considered and rejected. We studied the plunger very carefully, but that did not make us any the wiser.

'Gas,' said somebody, 'only a gas can push the plunger forward. How do we get an expanding gas inside the syringe – but not until we want it?' Then somebody else finally found the solution. Several drugs, such as 'Alkaseltzer', produce a gas when they come into contact with water. Behind the rubber plunger, there is a small hollow, where the charge is usually placed. We filled this hollow with 'Alkaseltzer', and sealed it with the head from a copper rivet, and some silicone. Between the plunger and the tailpiece, the syringe was filled with water. When the gun was fired, the rivet fell out because of the shock, and the 'Alkaseltzer' and the water came into contact. Carbon dioxide (CO_2) was produced and this pushed the plunger forward, injecting the drug into the animal. We tested the patent and it worked. We tried it again, and it worked again. We used it until we got a supply of charges somewhat later!

During the last few days before the expedition ship is due to sail from its harbour in northern Norway, the situation may seem very hectic, and at times even chaotic, as efforts are made to arrange everything at the last minute. But when we finally cast off and set sail, everything

Left
The Black Guillemot is a common bird in the Arctic. It breeds in small colonies on steep cliffs in coastal areas, and is often found wintering in open leads in the pack-ice.

seems to change. We soon get into a routine of work and rest. There is little that can disturb us, except bad weather and minor logistic problems. After a day's sailing, we pass Bjørnøya (Bear Island), and from now on we may expect the first signs of drift-ice. The air becomes colder, and there is often a thick fog. Birds hasten to and fro in all directions. Long rows of Brünnich's Guillemots, small swarms of Little Auks (*Plautus alle*) are sighted together with single Black Guillemots (*Cepphus grylle*), or

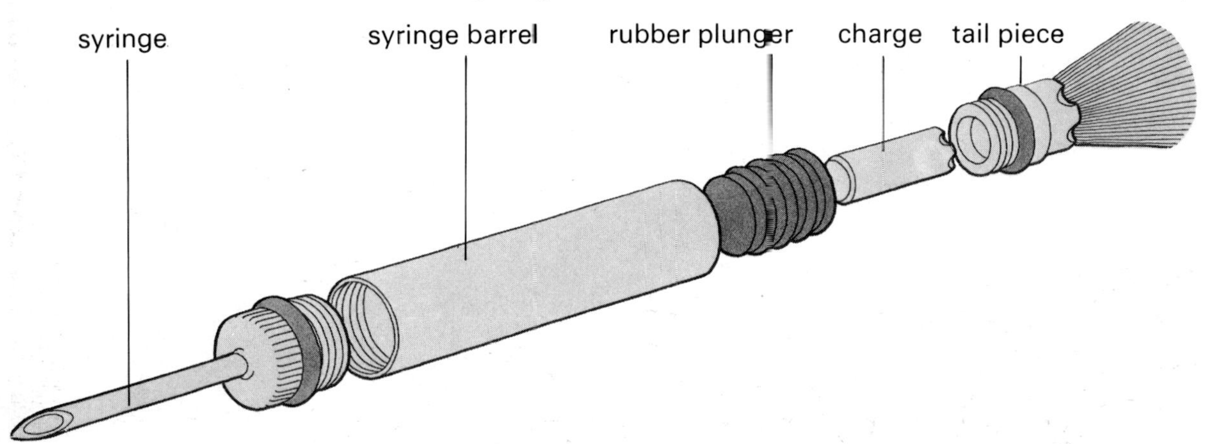

A typical syringe used in Polar Bear research.

The Norwegian sealer *'Polarulv'* (Polar Wolf) equipped as a research vessel. Note the cage on deck, where bears were kept during their recovery.

Puffins (*Fratercula arctica*). The Fulmars (*Fulmarus glacialis*) appear suddenly from nowhere. They sail in wide circles around the ship, down close to the water surface, sometimes so low that the tips of their wings even touch the water. They make a few strokes with their wings, then sail away again.

An icefloe suddenly comes floating out of the fog, washes along the ship's side, and disappears behind us. Soon there is so much ice around us that we have to slow down in order to avoid bumping into floes and so that we can manoeuver the vessel through the often narrow leads.

The fog lifts and soon afterwards we can observe far in all directions. The drift-ice is rather tight on our port side, because the prevailing winds from the west have packed it together. Birger Sørensen, the skipper, follows the ice edge and looks for an opening where he can sail into the ice. We are now in typical Polar Bear habitat and may meet bears at any time. I will describe a typical encounter.

A man is sent up in the crow's-nest in order to make observations. From up there he can see surprisingly far, registering changing ice conditions miles away. He can see open leads where the ship can sail, as well as flocks of birds and seals basking on the floes. He scans the ice and the horizon with his binoculars, but observations are difficult, for when the engine runs at half-speed the mast and the crow's-nest shake a great deal, which makes everything seen through the binoculars dance in front of his eyes. Now and then the ship's bow bumps into an icefloe and the observer is thrown against the sides of his tiny observatory. Bears are often difficult to see at a distance. The creamy or yellow colour of its fur is often difficult to distinguish from an old and somewhat dirty block of sea-ice. Also a low evening sun gives the ice a lot of colours and shadows; it is beautiful – but also fatiguing for the observer.

Some of us are standing in the steering house, which serves as clearing house, central command and information office, and besides all this it is the most popular place to be on a voyage like this. Here things are happening. The ever changing ice and weather situation are discussed. Decisions are made. If something happens the people in the steering house are the first ones to know. Now the mood is somewhat excited and alert, because we can expect Polar Bears any time. We can hear the man in the crow's-nest over the intercom, as there is a telephone up there. He stamps his boots on the platform in order to keep warm, and it rumbles in the loudspeaker. Then we hear a rattling as he moves the windshield for better protection against the icy wind. He hums and whistles in an effort to pass the time, because as time goes by and nothing interesting happens, things tend to become somewhat monotonous and boring up there. Then the whistling stops abruptly,

and everything is silent from 'the top'. When we glance through the window, we can see him staring through the binoculars to port. From the steering house we can see nothing but a chaos of ice and pressure ridges, because we are too low. Finally he speaks: 'I think we have a bear on the left .... No! It is two! No! Three! It is a female with two cubs!' Now it is time for some action. One man is sent below deck to wake up those who are off-duty and asleep below. The mate kicks the floor in the steering house which also is the roof in the galley, where others are passing the time by telling stories and sipping coffee. Soon everybody is up and on deck. Birger and I cling to the rope ladder under the crow's-nest and try to assess our position. 'We can chase them over the ice and into the sea,' I suggest. 'That is a difficult, and risky, operation,' answers Birger. He studies the ice carefully, and then he makes up his mind. 'We will sail into that narrow lead behind her. From there we can cut off their retreat, and get them out into open water. Then it will be easy – with the ship and the small boat working together.'

The ship is slowly turned around and the hunt begins. The first mate is steering. Here a skilled man is required as we go full

Left
From the crow's nest of a sealer, an observer has an excellent view of the of the surrounding pack-ice and leads. He can see seals and bears a good distance away, and can offer the helmsman valuable advice as to where to take the ship through the ice.

Below
Every landscape has its peculiar beauty – but few if any can match the pack-ice in summer, with its midnight sun and hazy pastel colours over the icefloes.

Right
When a swimming bear approaches a floe, it will put its forepaws on the ice, and jump out of the water with surprising speed and strength.

Opposite top
The bear is hoisted onboard the expedition vessel after being immobilized. There it will be marked and studied, and put in a cage to recover.

Opposite bottom
A big male Polar Bear onboard a research vessel in the Svalbard area. Scientists will mark the animal and take samples.

speed into the lead, among heavy floes and iceblocks, which could easily crush the hull at this speed. The bears have seen us. The cubs run up close to their mother as if seeking protection from her. She stretches her long neck and tries to get the scent from us. She is uneasy and bewildered, and is not sure how to tackle this new and very unfamiliar situation. Then she makes up her mind, and with the two cubs at her heels she heads for open water.

From then on it is an easy match. A small boat with an outboard engine is put on the water, and two men jump in. One takes care of the engine, and the other is responsible for the syringe gun. The bears are swimming towards an icefloe, and the small boat is close behind them. The female puts her large front paws on the ice and jumps out of the water. She stands on the ice for a moment – and that is enough for us. The man with the syringe gun fires. The aluminium syringe flies through the air, and hits the big carnivore on its left thigh. The bright red tailpiece is clearly visible and shows that it is a good hit. The bear growls, and then she heads for the water, her cubs following her. The men in the small boat follow, but not too close, because that may frighten her. After some time, the first signs of the drug's effect are shown. The bear's movements become slower, and she stumbles as she runs across a floe. As she climbs on to an icepan the small boat begins to circle around her and discourages her from jumping out in the water again. The female bear stands there and looks at the men. Then she yawns – another sign of the drug taking effect. Minutes later she is down, sleeping. It has taken almost twenty minutes from when she was hit until she went down. We could have got her down faster by using a bigger drug dosage, but then the side effects would have been more pronounced. With some experience, we prefer to give as little of the drug as possible, and wait instead.

The cubs keep close to their mother. We land the small boat very carefully at the icefloe, and climb on to the ice. Then we approach the animals slowly, avoiding any sudden movement and sharp voices. If we are very careful, we may get close enough to immobilize the cubs with the use of a hand syringe. But even if the cubs are relatively small, rarely weighing more than sixty kilograms (132 pounds) at six-months old, they are surprisingly strong and swift. We have learned that they can cause considerable harm with their sharp claws and teeth. Therefore, we have found it safest to immobilize them by means of a syringe mounted on a pole.

After all three bears have been drugged, they are hoisted on board the ship, for various studies. The adult bear is very heavy, but with the ship's boom it is an easy task to get it on deck. The cubs follow after; two men lift them over the reel and place them with their mother. Then we work on the animals following a routine which has become a fast and effective procedure. Each bear is weighed, and measurements are taken of its total length, girth etc. This enables us to tell something about its condition and size, and to correlate such information with the effect of the amount of drug given. Each bear is labelled with nylon tags in both ears. Previously we also used Monel-metal tags, but as we found that they caused some infection, we have stopped using them. Each tag has a number, and a return address, and a notice of a reward which is paid when the tag is recovered. But ear tags tend to fall off after some years. Therefore, a big tattoo, with the same cipher as on the tags, is punched inside the upper lip with a special pair of pliers. The tattoo marking will stay throughout the bear's life. A big dye number is rubbed into the fur on both sides. The number is

Right
Previously, Polar Bear cubs were captured by hunters, after their mothers had been killed, and were taken to the mainland where they were sold to zoos. Although often kept for months by the trappers, they rarely became as tame and easy to handle as Brown or Black Bear cubs.

Centre bottom
After one day the bear is completely recovered and can be released. The gate is opened and the bear can walk 'the plank' to freedom.

visible at long distances. It enables us to follow the bear's wanderings in the ice after they have been marked. Besides this – and perhaps more importantly – the bears are protected from hunters who operate in the same area as ourselves. They have been informed that hides from colour-marked bears are worthless, because the dye cannot be removed. It disappears only after the moult, when the coloured hairs are shed, and new hairs grow in place.

Some people have asked us if colour-marked bears are unable to catch seals. But Polar Bears usually take seals by surprise, and then their colour is of little importance. When they sneak up on their prey they often show their head and front and the colour-marked sides are not visible. Some people have asked us if colour-marked bears are shunned by others. But Polar Bears are generally solitary animals which seek each other's company only occasionally. The various markings do not seem to interfere with the bear's social life. Hundreds of 'controls' and recoveries over the years from more than a thousand marked Polar Bears are, however, the best proof that the marking techniques do not affect the animals and their way of living.

Blood samples are taken from the immobilized bears. Analyses of blood components can sometimes reveal genetic differences which can be used to distinguish different bear populations. Results from the blood analyses are compared with skull measurements and marking and recovery data. The total information can give us a knowledge which is crucial for the implementation of proper management controls for the bear population. A small reduced tooth, the so-called first premolar, is pulled from the lower jaw. No bigger than the tip of a match, it is not of importance to the animal, and is often lost from natural causes during the bear's lifetime. The animal is not harmed when the tooth is taken. In the laboratory, the tooth is sectioned and the annular rings or zones can be read, as with a tree-stump. Thus the animal's age can be determined. The population's age composition can tell us a lot about its status and about the hunting pressure.

Above
American and Canadian biologists have often used helicopters in their Polar Bear research. After the bear is immobilized, it is weighed under the helicopter.

When all this is over, the bears are put into the cage on deck. We keep them there until they are completely recovered, because we want to be sure that they are in good shape, when released. The recovery takes some time. The bears are at first able to lift their heads, and later to move their chest and forepaws. Some time later they can stand on all four legs, but movements are slow and careful. After a few hours the recovery is complete, and the animals behave normally, although we keep them for some time for observation. They rarely behave violently in the cage, but often they will try to find a way out. They are not aggressive, although we never move too close to the cage. If fed through the bars they will eat meat and blubber. Some bears cause us problems, however, although minor ones. Sometimes a caged bear finds a loose steel bar in one of the walls or the floor. Believing it may be a weak point and a way out, it starts moving the bar back and forth. The sharp sound from the banging metal is annoying. *Click, clack, click, clack* . . . it can go on for hours. The men below deck, who are trying to get some sleep, swear. The cook goes crazy, and everybody on deck seeks refuge, wherever they can avoid the sound. Finally we agree that such persistence deserves a reward. The gate is opened, and the bear is given its freedom. It jumps over the reel and down on to the ice. The ship continues its search for more bears, while our big passenger dozily walks over the icefloe, without even looking back at the ship.

In Alaska, the biologists of the Alaska Department of Fish and Game and the US Fish and Wildlife Service had begun to capture bears from helicopters in the pack-ice, with the assistance of a fixed-wing aircraft. The fixed-wing aircraft carried fuel for the helicopter and searched the pack-ice for signs of the bears, which were reported back to the helicopter. The helicopter could then move in without wasting time, and capture the bears using the syringe gun. Because of the manoeuvrability of the helicopter, it was easy to follow the bears even in rough terrain and to get close enough for a good shot. In

1967 thirty-one bears were captured, marked and studied. Other bear investigations off the Alaskan coast included aerial surveys and bear counts, age determination of bears, and reproductive studies. Alaskan biologists continued to collect samples and data from American Polar Bear hunters.

In the Soviet Arctic, Russian scientists continued their efforts to count dens in Wrangel Island. Aerial surveys were performed on a regular basis. During den counts, the scientists surveyed the actual areas both with aircraft and from the ground. Thus, they were able to obtain relatively accurate data on the number of Polar Bear dens in any given area, the litter sizes, and on when dens were being abandoned.

In Greenland, Danish scientists had not yet been able to begin their Polar Bear project. But skulls and other Polar Bear material were collected on a regular basis, and records were kept on the annual 'catch'.

However, simultaneously, there was an increasing concern about Polar Bear hunting throughout the world. In many regions, people who had previously used Polar Bear hides for clothing and other items, found it more beneficial to sell them and use modern textiles instead. A rapidly rising demand for hides increased the motivation for Polar Bear hunting which in turn stimulated a higher 'kill'. In 1966/67 more than 700 bears were taken in Canada alone. The number of hides sold annually had tripled in the post-war years, and the value had increased five fold. In Norway, some found it worthwhile to leave good jobs on the mainland to spend a winter as a trapper in Svalbard. Some hunters started to use snowmachines, and the summer hunting by tourists had developed into a profitable business. More than 300 bears were taken annually. In Alaska, where trophy hunting by means of aircraft was dominant, the number of bears killed rose from 139 in 1961 to 399 in 1966. Trophy hunters accounted for almost 90% of the 'take'. In Greenland an average of 126 Polar Bears a year were taken between 1960 and 1968. It is reasonable to assume that the rising prices on bear hides stimulated a similar increase in Polar Bear hunting in this part of the Arctic, as well. But as Greenland residents mainly used dog-sledges and traditional hunting methods, increased efforts are not so easily reflected in the total number of bears taken. We assume, however, that close to 150 bears were taken in Greenland each year.

In 1968, the IUCN followed up the recommendation from the First International Scientific Conference on the Polar Bear in Alaska in 1965 and acted in order to serve as coordinator for Polar Bear scientists and conservationists in the five Arctic nations. The IUCN invited Polar Bear experts to a meeting in Morges, Switzerland. The Danish delegate, Dr. Vibe, was unable to attend because of other urgent matters in Greenland. But Canada, Norway, USA, and USSR all sent their representatives. The experts reported on progress in research since 1965 and upon changes in management and conservation regulations. The participants agreed to standardize techniques and research methods, to exchange data and biological samples, and to cooperate on matters of bilateral and international concern. Research related to population discreteness and population sizes, migration, reproduction, and population dynamics was recommended to be given high priority. For example, the scientists agreed that Alaskan biologists on behalf of the group should work out age-determination methods, Canada should focus on Polar Bear skull morphology and geographical variation, and Norway on blood protein analysis.

Shortly afterwards, the IUCN established the Polar Bear Specialist Group under the auspices of its Survival Service Commission. The IUCN's specialist groups on endangered species were collecting and disseminating data, planning and coordinating research and forwarding its recommendations to the IUCN and other agencies concerned, so that they could take the necessary action in legislation. Representatives who participated in the 1968 meeting were appointed members of the new group, by their governments.

When the Polar Bear Specialist Group met again, in 1970, the delegates were able to report on considerable progress in research efforts. More than 450 bears had been captured, marked, and studied in Alaska, Canada, and Svalbard; there were also several recoveries. T. Manning in Canada had performed craniometric comparative investigations on Polar Bear

Wintering trappers who took Polar Bears in Svalbard used to sell their winter catch to one of the old and experienced tanneries in Tromso, Norway. Johan Storstad, in front of Polar Bear hides about to be tanned, had worked with seal and bear hides all his life, and knew all the old and famous trappers.

skulls from most parts of the Arctic, which revealed real differences between areas. On the basis of recovery data from marked bears and Manning's research results, it was agreed that Polar Bears did, in fact, belong to several different populations throughout their range. Analysis of hunting data and high recovery rates of marked bears indicated a heavy harvest in some regions, such as in Svalbard and Alaska. The group was concerned because of increasing human activity connected with oil exploration, transportation, etc. More than 1300 Polar Bears had been taken in the four countries which permitted Polar Bear hunting in 1970. The Soviet delegation proposed an appeal that called for a drastic curtailment of Polar Bear hunting over a five year period. This appeal was unanimously endorsed by the other group members. The participants of the meeting agreed that although Polar Bear hunting to some degree had been restricted on a national basis, such measures were not enough. The Polar Bear in particular required protection in international waters and pack-ice areas, where it roams for most of its lifetime. The appeal was forwarded to the IUCN Executive Council for consideration.

In 1972, Polar Bear research projects related to management were well under way in all the Arctic nations, except Denmark. But there was a realistic hope that Denmark would be able to launch a three-year Polar Bear program in 1973. Some 850 Polar Bears had been marked by the other countries, and recoveries confirmed the previous assumptions about the discreteness of Polar Bear populations. The scientists agreed that the Polar Bear was most definitely not a circumpolar wandering animal. Polar Bear conservation and management had to involve national and, in some cases, bilateral considerations with regard to its populations.

The Canadian Wildlife Service had expanded their research to include the High Arctic and the Beaufort Sea areas. This research program was closely linked with other institutions and included biologists, and graduate students in biology, ecology, and physiology. The Soviet Union were capturing Polar Bears in their denning areas and marking female bears which were found in the dens or about to leave their dens. One of the objectives with this study was to reveal whether females returned to the same denning area and, perhaps, the same den site from one year to another.

Above
Housing facilities are scarce in many Arctic regions, and travellers must depend upon tents. This party travels by traditional but safe means – skis and dog sledge.

Below
Small fixed-wing aircraft and helicopters have changed the method of travelling in the Arctic. They have made access to previously remote areas feasible, but they have also created new environmental and conservation problems.

LN-D

That same year, Norwegian research aimed at den surveys in Svalbard. Efforts were made to locate dens from the air and from the ground. Polar Bear dens are usually very difficult to find, except in early spring when the females emerge with their small cubs, and the den openings and tracks around the den can be seen. During midwinter, the den opening is sealed off by drifting snow, and there are no signs to indicate that a Polar Bear and her small cubs are sleeping only a few feet under the snow surface.

I had chartered two small fixed-wing aircraft with skis for the den surveys. Each plane carried two observers in addition to the pilot. Our pilots were very skilled, and had long experience of bush-flying in the Arctic and in the Norwegian mountains. They could manoeuver their small aircraft along hillsides, river-banks and other areas, where we could expect to find the dens. Although the pilots were flying at low altitudes and at a minimum speed, it was often necessary to survey a particular site repeatedly. We had to circle, pass the site again and again, until we were satisfied. Tracks were studied, and pictures were taken for later examination. Careful study of the tracks might tell us if we had found a maternity or a temporary den. The aircraft turned out to be feasible and efficient in large scale surveys, but it was also necessary to send field parties out. Small groups of two or three people were flown out into the field with skis and the necessary equipment, in order to survey regions of particular interest from the ground. Although I had to participate in the air surveys most of the time, I also used the opportunity to take part in ground surveys. I was involved in the survey of the southern part of Edgeøya – the region where I had stayed for more than a year in 1968/69, and which I knew particularly well. In early April, Ole, a fellow observer, and I landed at the station – 'Permafrost City' – on Andrée-tangen. The two buildings had not been used since the winter 1969/70 and it was strange and somewhat nostalgic for me to press the door open to the old trappers hut after so many years. This place was full of good memories. 1968/69 had been a year full of interesting field work, and exciting research – but also of long boring days as we waited for the storms to cease. There had been long journeys with the dog-teams, and hours of skiing along the ice-edge. We had appreciated the barren landscape around us and the polar night, but we had also dreamed about the green summer, and the beauty of everything we had left behind. During that year, our small group of four took on a new attitude towards nature, simply because we lived so close to it day after day. We found ourselves in an almost desert-like country, where

Opposite above
Small airplanes and snowmachines makes modern Arctic research effective and safe.

Opposite below
A team from the Danish *'Sirius'* sledge patrol in an east Greenland fjord. The members of the patrol are very skilled and experienced, and perform a difficult job in one of the most remote and harsh regions of the Arctic.

Arctic midnight sun.

beauty could be found in the pale pastel colours in the middle of the day, or in the ferocity of a snow-storm which forces you to stay inside for days, or in a magnificent aurora borealis which spreads across the entire midwinter night sky. The radio was our only link with civilization – the nearest community was several days travel away. Although we now and then heard about various calamities in the outer world over the radio, we discovered that the maintenance of our field gear and equipment, the success of a bread-baking venture or the well-being of our dogs, meant much more to us. During that winter, we became very good friends. Hardly a bad word fell, and if we disagreed, it was over trivial matters. Going back to the station brought all this back to life again. Little seemed to have changed. The worn-down furniture, and the utensils were there as before. The books were still on their shelves, and the familiar drawings and pictures were still on the walls. But the year which I remembered so well was behind me. Many things had changed since then, and if I tried to experience such a winter again, it would probably be very different.

From the station, Ole and I made long trips on skis to the surrounding areas, to look for Polar Bear dens. We went over to the little hut 'Blåsebelgen' (The Bellows), which lies just across Halvmåneøya, where I had so many exciting incidents with Polar Bears during that last winter. We saw tracks, and also came across a few bears – but no dens. After all, it was not so surprising. Previous investigations had shown that although Polar Bear dens had been found in that area before, they were relatively scarce. In 1969, we had only found half a dozen dens on Edgeøya and Barentsøya.

The drift-ice is a fascinating and changing landscape often with marvellous colours and shapes.

Between late March and early May, we flew almost 200 hours with the small aircraft, and field parties performed ground surveys on Edgeøya, Kong Karls Land, and Nordaustlandet. We found that the northern part of Nordaustlandet and the small archipelago Kong Karls Land were very important denning areas for Polar Bears. A total of eighty-four dens were found, of which twenty-six were on Nordaustlandet and forty-nine on Kong Karls Land. However, it was difficult to make accurate counts; riverbanks, hillsides and slopes were surveyed repeatedly, because weather and light conditions might affect counts and surveys. Drifting snow often filled up and covered dens shortly after they had been abandoned. We found that ground observation success was dependent upon topography as well as the weather and light conditions. Track observations around the dens and other signs indicated that about half the number of dens found were maternity dens. The rest were temporary dens, which had been used by single bears or family groups for shelter for a shorter or longer period.

In North America, American and Canadian bear researchers had managed to attach small radio transmitters to some bears. These transmitters were designed as collars embedded in fibre glass to fit

During winter the sea-ice freezes, and becomes more consolidated.

around the animal's neck. The signals were picked up by receivers mounted in aircraft. One major obstacle was the distance over which the radio signals could be obtained. In Alaska, signals from a 'bugged' bear could be picked up from a maximum range of fifty-five miles.

Physiological investigations on Polar Bears at Barrow included thermo-regulatory investigations at different activity levels and temperatures. American biologists had made efforts to estimate Polar Bear population size, productivity and mortality from hunting data. Based on this information, they concluded that there were about 5000 Polar Bears in Chukchi Sea and the Beaufort Sea pack-ice area. But the estimate had to be treated with great care, because of some assumptions and inaccurate data. American biologists had also tried to survey and count bears in the pack by the use of infra-red photographic equipment, mounted in aircraft. But success was limited, although more efforts should be made to develop this particular technique.

The Russians were concentrating their efforts on Wrangel Island and on den studies there. Den counts were performed using aircraft and field parties. The counts revealed that Wrangel Island was one of the Arctic regions where Polar Bear dens were most abundant. Here dens were sometimes found only a short distance apart. The Russian Polar Bear investigations included studies of den location and structure, behaviour of female bears and cubs, studies of non-breeding bears in the Wrangel Island area and estimates of Polar Bear numbers. Russian biologists had also begun to capture and mark live bears. They immobilized females by using the syringe gun, while the animals were still in their dens or about to leave them.

The Danes launched their first major effort in Polar Bear research in 1973. Field studies were concentrated on the east coast of Greenland, between early-April and mid-May. The objective of the Danish research was to count dens, to perform population estimates, to study bear migration, and to make observations.

Polar Bear research is now well under the way in all five Arctic nations, on a continuous basis. In recent years, the priorities may have changed somewhat. Up until now, physiological and ethological aspects have had low priority in most Polar Bear programs. It is necessary to study the contents of toxic chemical components from industry and agriculture such as polychlorinated hydrocarbons (PCB) and heavy metals which are already present in Polar Bear tissue throughout the Arctic. Also it is important to discover whether there are separate Polar Bear stocks which live almost exclusively on the polar pack-ice, and which den in the ice hummocks and pressure ridges on the polar ice. One of the things which is receiving particular attention now is the development of a computer simulation model for Polar Bears. Although the scientists for the time being do not expect a model to be very predictive for management and conservation purposes, they hope it will yield valuable information as to research needs and priorities, and help standardize the collection of data, and rationalize future international Polar Bear research.

The recent changes in the management

and conservation of the Polar Bear throughout the Arctic, is above all a result of the close cooperation between scientists and legislators concerned with the problem. The Polar Bear Specialist Group members have close contact with legislators and politicians in their respective countries, which permits efficiency and fast reactions when necessary. When the group meets, their working sessions are closed in order to permit free discussions and constructive criticism, without the dangers of misunderstandings and wrong quotations by others. The group members are all good friends and most of them have worked together in the field and the laboratory, for many years. The dialogue between the Polar Bear specialists and the IUCN staff members has always been – and is – very good.

After the Soviet delegation urged a curtailment of the Polar Bear harvest throughout the Arctic at the 1970 Group meeting, the Group and the IUCN together sought to find an acceptable solution for that demand. These efforts resulted in an international agreement which was signed in 1973.

Protection and the future

As previously mentioned the Soviet delegation to the IUCN Polar Bear Specialist Group forwarded an appeal in 1970 which pointed out that Polar Bear populations in various countries had not essentially increased in spite of various restrictions in Polar Bear hunting, and that rational management had to be based upon current research programs on Polar Bears undertaken in each Arctic country. A moratorium of at least five years would promote the restoration of Polar Bear populations in various parts of the Arctic.

On the basis of this appeal, the IUCN in 1972 prepared a draft proposal for an international convention on the Polar Bear, which was aimed at a more effective protection of the species. The delegates at the 1972 Polar Bear Specialist Group meeting, although officially nominated by their countries, felt that they had no power to speak for their governments. But they reviewed the draft as 'professionals', and advised IUCN on that background. The group also presented a resolution, which urged a prohibition of Polar Bear hunting on the high seas, including the area of the circumpolar pack-ice, and a better protection of national denning and feeding areas.

The IUCN was asked to prepare another draft on the basis of these discussions, and to circulate it to group members. After discussing this new draft with their respective authorities, the group members reported about the results at a short meeting in Banff, Canada, September 1972. The IUCN proposal had got a favourable reception, and the impression was that there was a common platform for an international agreement.

Norway offered to host consultations on this topic between the five Arctic nations, and to be depositary for an eventual agreement for the protection of the Polar Bear. The Norwegian government called a conference for the preparation of such an agreement, to be based on the recommendations and proposals from the IUCN and its Polar Bear Specialist Group. The conference was arranged for 13–15 November 1973. There, the discussions were finalized, and an agreement was signed by Canada, Denmark, Norway, and USA. The USSR signed in early 1974. By December 1974, Norway and Canada had ratified the agreement as did the USSR in 1976. The remaining two countries are expected to follow soon. The IUCN will urge nations which might have an interest and capability in hunting Polar Bears and dealing in the trade of skins, to abide by the provisions of the agreement.

According to this agreement, the taking of Polar Bears is prohibited by the contracting parties, i.e. the five Arctic nations, except: for *bona fide* scientific purposes; for conservation purposes; to prevent serious disturbance of the management of other living resources; by local people using traditional methods in the exercise of their traditional rights; or wherever Polar Bears have or might have been subject to taking by traditional means.

The skins and other items of value from bears taken for conservation purposes, or nuisance bears, shall not be available for commercial purposes under the terms of the agreement.

Among other things, the agreement's Article 5 prohibits export, import, and traffic within the contracting nations of Polar Bears or Polar Bear parts and products taken in violation of the agreement. Article 7 requires the contracting parties to conduct national research programs on Polar Bears, particularly relating to the conservation and management of the species. They are to coordinate such research and consult with other parties on the management of migrating Polar Bear populations, and to exchange information on research and management programs, research results and data on bears taken.

With this agreement the Polar Bear has been granted an effective protection

A young and curious Polar Bear on an icefloe.

nationally as well as internationally, initially for a period of five years from 1976. The agreement will remain in force after that period, unless one of the parties requests termination.

Those nations which have Polar Bears within their jurisdictions will have to study the impact of these new protective measures upon the Polar Bear population. In five years' time, when the agreement is to be reviewed, new information must be available to the decision-makers. Den studies and reproductive studies, as well as renewed population estimates, must have special attention. Although the Polar Bear as a species is protected now, the

National delegates to the IUCN Polar Bear Specialist Group Meetings

Year	Denmark	Canada	USA	Norway	USSR
1968	C. Vibe	C. Jonkel A. H. Macpherson	J. W. Brooks J. W. Lentfer	T. Larsen M. Norderhaug	A. G. Bannikov S. M. Uspensky
1970	C. Vibe				
1970	C. Vibe	C. Jonkel A. H. Macpherson	J. W. Brooks J. W. Lentfer	T. Larsen M. Norderhaug	A. A. Kistshchinski S. M. Uspensky
1972 I	C. Vibe	C. Jonkel A. H. Macpherson	J. W. Brooks J W. Lentfer	T. Larsen M. Norderhaug	A. A. Kistshchinski S. M. Uspensky
1972 II	C. Vibe	C. Jonkel G. Kolenosky	J W. Brooks J W. Lentfer	T. Larsen M. Norderhaug	A. A. Kistshchinski
1974	C. Vibe	C. Jonkel G. Kolenosky	J Lentfer	T. Larsen E. Reimers	S. M. Uspensky

J. Tener from Canada has acted as chairman of the meetings. The secretariat has been headed by the Executive Officer of the IUCN Survival Service Commission, Miss Moira A. G Warland (1968–72) and Mr. Anthony J. Mence (1974–).

Above
A typical Eskimo trapping area in the Canadian Northwest Territories.

Opposite
Bears are curious – but you should not let them come too close. In this case there is little danger, although the distance is less than five metres (sixteen feet), because the photographer is sitting in a boat.

scientists agree that it is important to give ample protection to its habitat as well. For that reason, the Polar Bear Specialist Group members are preparing a Polar Bear ecology map, which will show Polar Bear abundance in various areas at different times of the year, migratory routes, denning areas, feeding areas, etc. Such a map is difficult to make because quantitative information is not immediately comparable from one region to another, due to different census methods and investigation techniques. But, through their close contacts with colleagues in other countries, most of the Polar Bear workers have to a large extent joined forces in the field. This will undoubtedly facilitate the work.

The future

When the First International Scientific Conference on the Polar Bear was arranged in 1965, the Polar Bear was listed in the Red Data Book of the IUCN as an endangered species. As new regulations were introduced, which give the species adequate protection throughout its range, IUCN transferred the species to its 'Amber' list, which means that although not in immediate danger, it is still under threat from serious adverse factors throughout its range. The data sheet on the Polar Bear now reads: 'There is still cause for concern, but not alarm if international accord can be reached on protective and management measures'. With the ratification of the 1973 agreement that requirement seems to have been met with and the future seems promising for the Polar Bear.

As the Polar Bear has been more effectively protected, there has been a decline in hides offered for sale throughout the world. In the USSR and Norway, Polar Bears are totally protected, whilst in Greenland and in Alaska only indigenous people can hunt Polar Bears and even then mostly for their own use. Limited hunting for sport can be performed in Canada. Local people holding a permit are sometimes allowed to sell it to a sport hunter, but he must still be guided by Eskimos and travel by dog-team. But as Polar Bear rugs become increasingly scarce, prices rise. During the last few years, prices of good hides have increased several hundred per cent in some places. On the black market, up to $10 000 was paid for a good pelt in 1973–74. More recently the prices have dropped again. At the 1974–75 auctions in Canada and Denmark, an average price of less than $600 was paid for hides offered for sale.

Opposite top
The Polar Poppy (*Papaver radicatum*) is one of the most beautiful flowers to be found in the Arctic. It often grows in areas with signs of erosion and where one would expect nothing would be able to grow at all.

Opposite below left
Saxifrage is a common plant in the Arctic. It often covers the tundra in a thick red carpet, which characterizes the landscape for miles.

Opposite below right
Flowers on the Arctic tundra – lush, colourful and beautiful.

Below
Lichens, in surprisingly strong colours, are found where you would expect nothing to grow.

Some markets have closed, because of the Convention on the International Trade in Endangered Species of Wild Fauna and Flora, which prohibits the uncontrolled import and export of Polar Bear hides. The US Marine Mammal Act of 1972 bans the import of Polar Bear hides into the US, and prohibits the sale of rugs and hides from Polar Bears taken within US territory. A tagging system has been introduced in many countries, to prevent the illegal tanning and sale of contraband Polar Bear hides.

Scientists and conservationists have learned that it is normally not enough to just protect plants and animal species alone. It is just as important to restrict the many human activities which may cause both biological and environmental damage. The ultimate goal is to protect the ecosystems with viable populations of plants and animals. This can be done primarily by protecting large areas where the life systems, natural habitats and landscapes remain relatively undisturbed. Such protected areas are most commonly classified as national parks, nature reserves, or game reserves, depending upon the regulations and various protective measures introduced. Some such areas offer a suitable refuge for Polar Bears, or have been established with particular reference to the protection of the Polar Bear. Ontario, for example, established a Polar Bear Provincial Park of more than 15 000 square kilometres (5790 square miles) in Hudson Bay/Cape Henrietta Maria area. The park was established primarily for the protection of Polar Bear denning sites, and the intention is to leave the area in its natural state. The Soviet Union has protected several areas within the Wrangel Island Republic Reserve. They include the Drem-Head Mountains, Hawaii Hills and the East Plateau, all of which are important Polar Bear denning areas. Regulations are very strict and most human activities are prohibited in the areas. Also in Svalbard, large protected areas have recently been set aside. Of special interest may be the Northeast and Southeast Svalbard Nature Reservations, which cover Nordaustlandet, Kvitøya, Kong Karls Land, Barentsøya and Edgeøya and several smaller islands, i.e. the part of Svalbard which is found east of Hinlopenstretet and Storfjorden. These islands, totalling more than 21 000 square kilometres (8100 square miles) are also the most important Polar Bear habitat in Svalbard, and bears almost exclusively den within the reservations. The most recent protective measure has been launched by Denmark. In 1974, a huge national park was proclaimed in northeast Greenland, between Hall Basin in the north and Liverpool Land in the south. With its 700 000 square kilometres (270 000 square miles) this park is the world's largest, and it gives ample protection for

Bears which are pursued, will often seek refuge on an iceberg or a mountain. They are able to climb very steep hill-sides with surprising speed.

the High Arctic ecosystems in east Greenland including the east Greenland Polar Bear population. In addition a game reserve has been established in Melville Bay, among other things for the protection of the Polar Bear on northwest Greenland.

With the severe temperature and weather conditions that prevail in the polar regions few plant and animal species can exist and function. Some species may occur in great numbers, but if they are reduced, they may have great difficulties in recovering. If a species disappears, others may not be able to take its place. Individuals and populations reproduce and build more slowly than in temperate regions. Plant and animal populations may take a long time to recover after damage. The plant cover in perma-frost areas, which is essential to prevent soil erosion, is very vulnerable and may take decades to heal. Pollutants may take a very long time to break down into less harmful components. It is only recently that the ecosystems and life forms of the polar regions have been extensively studied. But scientists have discovered that in the Arctic and in Antarctica they may find systems which are relatively undisturbed, and where the relationships and interactions between organisms can be better studied than on lower latitudes. But at the same time as we have learned more about the complexity of the polar ecosystems, we have simultaneously developed a technology which makes it possible for us to explore these remote parts of our planet. The polar regions are no longer inaccessible to Man. With strong ships, aircraft and snowmachines able to provide ready access to the most remote areas, there may be serious problems ahead which may have a massive impact in the High Arctic regions where the landscapes, as well as the flora and fauna have remained undisturbed for centuries. Oil and gas have been found in many parts of the Arctic, as on the North Alaskan coast, and in the High Canadian Arctic and with an increasing demand for fossil fuels and raw materials for the industrialized world, there are intensive efforts to explore such resources wherever they may be. Airstrips, roads and pipelines are being constructed, camps and small towns built. Some of these constructions are huge, and will have a serious impact on the polar nature, resulting in a possible degradation of life forms and natural habitats. One example is the so-called Trans-Alaskan pipeline, which will transport oil across Alaska from Prudhoe Bay to Valdez. Another very ambitious project is the construction of roads, pipelines and other facilities through the Canadian Mackenzie River Valley. Oil exploration has already been carried out in Svalbard for many years, and there is an interest in starting oil

Arctic Hares (*Lepus arcticus*) are fully adapted to a life in a cold environment. They have short ears, and thick fur on their legs and body.

exploration and drilling in northeast Greenland. As more wells are drilled and more pipelines or tankers transport the oil out of the Arctic, there are also increasing risks of massive oil spills. We already know of the catastrophic effects of blowouts and spills from supertankers in other parts of the world. We also know that similar accidents will probably be far more serious in the Arctic, because of the permafrost, the lack of drainage, the extremely slow degradation of the oil components in the cold and other factors not yet fully understood. Oil may be spread over huge tundra areas, and effect plant and animal life for years. The oil and its by-products may also be trapped in the sea among floes or under the ice, where it can cause very serious damage to the plankton production and to the fish, birds, and mammals which live upon it. There is a must, that when oil, gas and various minerals are exploited in the Arctic, every possible precaution should be taken, to avoid ecological disasters.

Parallel to the discovery of vast amounts of non-renewable resources in the Arctic, the polar regions have become new and exciting goals for tourists and naturalists from all over the world. People have discovered landscapes, life forms and beauty which have been unknown to most of them. They find a land full of barren landscapes, with wild and rugged mountains, endless tundra and huge glaciers. They discover that polar lands may have a surprisingly rich flora and fauna: flowers of many kinds and colours, which are sometimes so abundant that they cover the ground like carpets; huge cliffs with thousands and thousands of breeding seabirds; strange animals like Muskoxen and seals, or curious animals which have never encountered humans before and therefore show little or no fear of them. Not surprisingly, travels to the polar regions have become increasingly popular. The fact that such trips are expensive because of the logistics involved does not seem to be any major obstacle to potential visitors.

We should all be happy that more and more people discover and appreciate the polar nature and its peculiar beauty. The philosophy should not be to seal off areas of particular interest or beauty to visitors. Nature should not be protected from Man,' but should be for the benefit of Man. We realize that clean air and water and healthy biological renewable resources are essential for our survival. But we also need beauty, space and undisturbed nature for our mental and physical health. The polar regions have been classified as the last paradises on planet Earth – still not significantly altered or ruined by Man. In an increasingly more industrialized world, we and our descendants cannot afford to lose them.

The Arctic Fox (*Alopex lagopus*) is a common and very friendly little creature. It is found in most of the northern polar regions, where it lives on lemmings, rodents, birds and their eggs. In winter it often follows Polar Bears out on to the pack-ice and scavenges upon prey left by the bears.

Bibliography

The following publications are suggestions for readers who want to know more about the life of the Polar Bear and the research that has been carried out.

Arctic Institute of North America, 1966. *A Polar Bear bibliography*. Washington DC. 25pp.

Bruemmer, F., 1969. *The Polar Bear*. Canadian Geographical Journal. 78(3).

Freuchen P., Salomonsen F., 1959. *The Arctic year*. Cape, London. 44pp.

Herrero, S., 1972. *Bears – their biology and management. Papers and proceedings of the International Conference on Bear Research and Management, Calgary, Alberta, Canada 6–9 Nov. 1970.* IUCN Publications New Series No. 23. 371pp.

IUCN Survival Service Commission, 1970. *Polar Bears. Proceedings of the 2nd Working Meeting of the Polar Bear Specialist Group.* IUCN Publications New Series, Supplementary Papers No. 29. 88pp.

IUCN Survival Service Commission, 1972. *Polar Bears. Proceedings of the 3rd Working Meeting of the Polar Bear Specialist Group.* IUCN Publications New Series, Supplementary Papers No. 35. 97pp.

IUCN Survival Service Commission, 1976. *Polar Bears. Proceedings of the 5th Working Meeting of the Polar Bear Specialist Group.* IUCN Publications New Series, Supplementary Paper No. 42. 105pp.

Jonkel, C. J., 1969. *Polar Bear research in Canada.* Canadian Wildlife Series Progress Notes No. 13. 10pp.

Larsen, T., 1971. *Polar Bear: Lonely nomad of the north.* National Geographic Magazine 139(4): 574–590.

Larsen, T., 1972. *Isbjornliv.* Cappelen, Oslo. 174pp.

Lønø, O., 1970. *The Polar Bear in the Svalbard area.* Norsk Polarinstitutt Skrifter nr. 149. 103pp.

Manning, T. H., 1971. *Geographical variation in the Polar Bear.* Canadian Wildlife Service Report Series No. 13. 27pp.

Nansen, F., 1925. *Hunting and adventure in the Arctic.* Duffield & Co. 462pp. (Translated from 'Blant sel og Bjorn').

Pedersen, A., 1945. *Der Eisbär.* Verbreitung und Lebensweise. E. Brunn & Co. København. 166pp.

Pelton, M. R., Lentfer J. W., Folk G. E., 1976. *Bears – their biology and Management. Papers of the Third International Conference on Bear Research and Management, Binghampton, New York, USA and Moscow, USSR June 1974.* IUCN Publications New Series No. 40. 467pp.

Perry, R., 1966. *The world of the Polar Bear.* Cassell & Co. London. 195pp.

Sokolov, V. E., 1973. *Ecology and morphology of the Polar Bear* 'Nauka' publishing house, Moscow. 162pp.

Stefansson, V., 1921. *The friendly Arctic.* Macmillan, London. 784pp.

Stonehouse, B., 1971. *Animals of the Arctic. The ecology of the far North.* Ward Lock, London. 172pp.

US Department of the Interior, 1965. *Proceedings of the First International Scientific Meeting on the Polar Bear, Fairbanks, Alaska 6–10 September 1965.* US Government Printing House. 72pp.

Uspensky, S. M., 1973. *Rodina Belych Medvedej (Home of the Polar Bear).* 'Mysl' publishing house, Moscow. 176pp.

Uspensky, S. M., 1977. *Belyj Medved' (The Polar Bear).* 'Nauka' publishing house, Moscow. 80pp.

Vibe, C., 1967. *Arctic animals in relation to climatic fluctuations.* Meddelelser om Grønland 170(5). 227pp.

The Arctic is often harsh presenting difficult conditions for both plants and animals. Yet it is one of the few relatively unspoilt areas of the World with a unique beauty and wildness which modern man needs now more than ever before.

Index

Page numbers in italics refer to illustrations.

Acknowledgements

Photographs
Ian Bakkerud 14–15; Annemor Brekke 11 bottom; Fred Breummer, Montreal 22, 31 bottom, 32, 33, 37 top, 38–39, 40–41, 44, 45 top, 46–47, 49 top, 55, 87 bottom right; Bruce Coleman Ltd, Uxbridge – Jen and Des Bartlett 31 top; Bruce Coleman Ltd – Nicholas De Vore 34, 63, 84; Bruce Coleman Ltd – N. R. Lightfoot 37 bottom; Bruce Coleman Ltd – Norman Owen Tomalin 57 bottom; Bruce Coleman Ltd – J. Van Wormer 27 bottom; John Davies, Bristol 45 centre, 45 bottom; J. Faro 42–43 top; Hamlyn Group Picture Library 13 top left, 13 top right, 13 bottom, 39 top; Olaf Hjeljord 7, 59 top; Thor Larsen, title spread, 9 bottom, 21, 23, 25, 27 top, 30 top, 30 centre, 42, 49 centre, 50, 50–51, 54–55, 56–57 top, 56–57 bottom, 57 top, 59 top centre, 59 bottom centre, 59 bottom, 60–61, 64, 65, 66 bottom, 67, 68, 69 top, 69 bottom, 71 top, 72–73 top, 72–73 bottom, 74, 75 top, 75 bottom, 76–77 top, 76–77 bottom, 78–79, 83, 85, 86, 87 top, 90, 91, 93, endpapers; Jack W. Lentfer 24, 52, 66 top, 73; Mansell Collection, London 17 bottom, 18–19; Magnar Norderhaug 42–43 bottom; Svein Oppegaard 8, 9 top, 53, 70, 71 bottom, 78; Radio Times Hulton Picture Library, London 17 top, 17 centre, 20 top, 20 bottom, 54 top; Dr. Hugh Simpson, Glasgow 11 top, 12, 39, 80–81; Jørn Thomassen 35, 87 bottom left; Christian Vibe 88–89.